A Manager's Guide to the
New World of Work

The Digital Future of Management Series from MIT Sloan Management Review

Edited by Paul Michelman

A Manager's Guide to the New World of Work

The Most Effective Strategies for Managing People, Teams, and Organizations

MIT Sloan Management Review

Management Review

The MIT Press
Cambridge, Massachusetts
London, England

This book was set in Stone Serif and Stone Sans by Jen Jackowitz. Printed and bound in the United States of America.

Library of Congress Cataloging-in-Publication Data is available.

ISBN: 978-0-262-53944-9

10   9   8   7   6   5   4   3   2   1

Contents

6

Does AI-Flavored Feedback Require a Human Touch?
Michael Schrage

7

What Managers Can Gain from Anonymous Chats
Ryan Bonnici

8

Are Your Employees Driven to Digital Distraction?
Brian Solis

II Managing Teams

9

Get Things Done with Smaller Teams
Chris DeBrusk

10

Why Teams Still Need Leaders
Lindred Greer, interviewed by Frieda Klotz

11

Why Teams Should Record Individual Expectations
Ken Favaro and Manish Jhunjhunwala

12

Collaborate Smarter, Not Harder
Rob Cross, Thomas H. Davenport, and Peter Gray

13

Improving the Rhythm of Your Collaboration
Ethan Bernstein, Jesse Shore, and David Lazer

Series Foreword

Books in the Digital Future of Management series draw from the print and web pages of *MIT Sloan Management Review* to deliver expert insights and sharply tuned advice on navigating the unprecedented challenges of the digital world. These books are essential reading for executives from the world's leading source of ideas on how technology is transforming the practice of management.

Paul Michelman
Editor in chief
MIT Sloan Management Review

Introduction: Managing Today for the Future

Welcome to the new world of work.

In this book, we highlight the smartest new thinking and research on how leaders are navigating the unprecedented challenges of the new digital workplace, an environment in which technology's presence knows no bounds. You'll find stories and insights from companies that are charting new courses—what they've tried, what's worked, what's failed, and what they've learned.

In part I, "Managing People," we look at the strategies that organizations use to help employees and managers adapt to a fast-changing world. How do companies help employees step away from always being connected? How do we as individuals embrace the technology that competes for part of our jobs? How do organizations help employees build the skills that will keep them employable?

In this section, we present the following chapters on current challenges and solutions:

- **Train Your People to Think in Code.** David Waller (Oliver Wyman Labs) argues that organizations need to solve problems with reusable solutions to avoid reengineering the process from the ground up—and that the best way to do so is to make code the natural language for sharing analysis across the business.

- **Leisure Is Our Killer App.** Psychologist Adam Waytz (Kellogg School of Management at Northwestern University) lays out why the capacity to let our minds wander can give humans a surprising edge against advancing technologies in the battle for jobs.

- **Self-Reports Spur Self-Reflection.** Angela Duckworth (University of Pennsylvania) details how carefully crafted questionnaires asking people to rate themselves can be a tool for self-reflection and self-development, making conversations about character easier to have by laying the foundations of a shared language. Self-awareness, as she notes, is one step toward self-actualization.

- **Career Management Isn't Just the Employee's Job.** (both of the Wharton People Analytics initiative) draw from their team's research into how organizations are helping their people build better careers and argue that analytics can be creatively used for career mapping and for identifying passive internal candidates.

- **Can We Really Test People for Potential?** Reb Rebele (Wharton People Analytics initiative) explains that people metrics are hard to get right—in part because there can be even more variation within one individual's personality than there is from person to person.

- **Does AI-Flavored Feedback Require a Human Touch?** Michael Schrage (MIT Initiative on the Digital Economy) notes that direct managerial involvement both complements and competes with data-determined performance reviews.

- **What Managers Can Gain from Anonymous Chats.** Ryan Bonnici (G2 Crowd) writes that managers who are brave enough to collect anonymous feedback from staff can use that information to help retain great employees, boost productivity, and build greater engagement.

- **Are Your Employees Driven to Digital Distraction?** Brian Solis (Altimeter) lays out both big-picture strategies (such as rethinking open offices) and individual practices (such as concentrating on a single task for 25 minutes followed by a break of 5 minutes) for maintaining focus in an ever-distracting digital world.

In part II, "Managing Teams," we explore the way digital tools affect our work in groups. With so many tools available, both for connecting people and for analyzing the work they do together, what is the right role for a manager? How do managers help teams do their best work?

In this part, we highlight specific approaches and suggestions:

- **Get Things Done with Smaller Teams.** Chris DeBrusk (Oliver Wyman) describes 10 ways that smaller, more agile teams can achieve greater productivity for the organization—from compartmentalizing large, complex problems into separate, achievable pieces that a small team can easily take on and overdeliver, to actively managing away from having "indispensable" people in change and transformation projects.

- **Why Teams Still Need Leaders.** In a Q&A, Lindred (Lindy) Greer, associate professor of management and organizations at the University of Michigan's Ross School of Business, argues that when people collaborate remotely, good leaders both promote autonomy and use hierarchy to keep teams moving in the same direction.

- **Why Teams Should Record Individual Expectations.** Ken Favaro (act2) and Manish Jhunjhunwala (Trefis) write about their own experience developing a basic spreadsheet to capture the individual volume, price, and revenue expectations for both sides of a new partnership deal and converting that spreadsheet into an interactive dashboard viewable to investors, directors, top executives, and employees involved in the partnership.

- **Collaborate Smarter, Not Harder.** Rob Cross (Babson College), Thomas H. Davenport (Babson), and Peter Gray (McIntire School of Commerce at the University of Virginia) explain how the benefits of understanding patterns of collaboration can be reaped in all kinds of organizations, and that using analytics to make collaborative activities more transparent helps companies identify and exploit previously invisible drivers of revenue production, innovation, and employee effectiveness.

- **Improve the Rhythm of Your Collaboration.** Ethan Bernstein (Harvard Business School), Jesse Shore (Boston University's Questrom School of Business), and David Lazer (Northeastern University) note that as collaborative tools make interaction cheaper and more abundant, opportunities to think without interaction are becoming scarcer and more expensive. They explain why alternating between always-on connectivity and heads-down focus is essential for problem solving.

In part III, "Managing Organizations," we zoom out and look at the big picture. What are the trends and opportunities about the new world of work that leaders need to know about and plan for? How do new expectations around the customer experience—that it be fast, easy, and mobile-ready—influence the way organizations are structured? How should a leader be thinking about the management of people and operations overall?

Here we lay out the big questions for managing in the digital age:

- **Reframing the Future of Work.** Jeff Schwartz (Deloitte Consulting), John Hagel III (Deloitte's Center for the Edge), Maggie Wooll (Center for the Edge), and Kelly Monahan (Deloitte Services LP) explore the opportunity that comes when companies expand their notions of value beyond cost to the company—and shift their focus from solely the company to the customer, workforce, and company.

- **It's Time to Rethink the IT Talent Model.** Will Poindexter and Steve Berez (both with Bain & Company's Technology and Agile Innovation practices) explain why, to have a truly effective digital organization, companies have to fix the speed bumps that slow down the rapid progress of agile software development. That means overcoming three impediments that work against agile in most organizations: rigid architecture, poor talent management, and lack of a product mindset.

- **New Ways to Gauge Talent and Potential.** Josh Bersin (Bersin by Deloitte) and Tomas Chamorro-Premuzic (Manpower-Group) examine how, while most organizations still rely on traditional hiring methods such as résumé screenings and job interviews, a new generation of assessment tools is quickly gaining traction—and making talent identification more precise and less biased.

- **Pioneering Approaches to Re-skilling and Upskilling.** Lynda Gratton (London Business School) writes that everyone, whatever their age, will eventually have to spend time either re-skilling (learning new skills for a new position) or upskilling (learning current tasks more deeply). She argues that individuals' commitment to keeping their skills competitive will work only if corporations step up to make this possible.

- **How Managers Can Best Support a Gig Workforce.** Adam Roseman (Steady) notes that the unpredictability that many contingent workers face, such as differing income from month to month and limited or no work benefits, makes their lives a real struggle. Managers can help alleviate stress with three steps: scheduling workers at least two weeks out, providing training, and offering small loans in times of financial emergency.

- **Unleashing Innovation with Collaboration Platforms.** Massimo Magni (Bocconi University) and Likoebe Maruping (J. Mack Robinson College of Business at Georgia State University) write that their study of over 600 team members, team coordinators, and managers who use collaboration platforms suggests two key factors that affect how much of a benefit teams get from collaboration platforms: how well the collaboration platform supports activities needed to integrate team knowledge despite geographically different locations, and whether team leaders can establish conditions that foster knowledge integration in a digital environment.

And finally, in part IV, we share *MIT Sloan Management Review*'s case study, produced in collaboration with McKinsey & Company, into how IBM reimagined talent and performance management beginning in 2015. Its end goal: higher levels of employee engagement that would allow the organization to fully engage its people in a business transformation.

The case study dives deep into the digitalization possibilities of performance management:

- **Rebooting Work for a Digital Era.** Until recently, IBM's performance management system followed a traditional approach that revolved around year-long cycles, ratings, and annual reviews. David Kiron and Barbara Spindel explore how, after recognizing that this model was holding back the organization, IBM reimagined its performance management system to cultivate a high-performance culture with a system of shorter-term goals, continuous feedback, and regularly updated milestones.

There is no one map or app that can guide us through all the challenges of the fast-evolving world of work. There are simply too many unknowns and too much yet to learn and experience. But we do believe that this book will help point you in the right direction.

Enjoy the journey!

I

Managing People

1

Train Your People to Think in Code

David Waller

Most companies still equate *doing analysis* with writing formulas in spreadsheets. But that's an outdated approach. Now that organizations must cater to and engage with millions of individual customers, not just a handful of segments, they must create reusable solutions to avoid reengineering problems from the ground up again and again. And they want to benefit from the latest advances in machine learning and AI. They can't do any of that if they simply throw regressions at whatever challenges they face. In short, companies need to retrain their people to think in code, not just formulas.

This requires a significant shift in mindset. Many managers see code as the province of data scientists and the IT department. But organizations that make it the natural language for diffusing analysis across units, teams, and functions will benefit in three ways. First, thinking in code allows companies to cleanly separate data from analysis of the data, which means different teams can focus independently on the areas where they need to improve, leading to faster progress all around. Second, code is easy to trace, modify, share, and reuse—the entire open-source movement rests on this idea. By adopting key principles of software development, such as version control, enterprise teams can be more efficient and collaborative as updates to files are tracked throughout their lifetime and changes can be reversed easily.

Third, breakthroughs in machine learning and AI are implemented in code. By cloning the code researchers are using, individuals throughout the organization can gain access to state-of-the-art techniques in analysis, quickly and for free. What must managers do to move their workforce from formulas to code? I've observed that leaders in this area take the following steps.

Tear Down the 'Tower of Babel'

Communication barriers get in the way of idea sharing and collaboration. This is not just true for text exchanges and spoken conversations—it's equally true for code. But having to recast ideas in several programming languages requires additional expertise and can be cognitively demanding.

What's the solution?

Select at most two analytical programming languages, but ideally one, as a companywide standard—something everyone can "speak." To be clear: No single language is perfect for every situation, and reasonable people can disagree on the choice of standard, so teams should prepare for familiar change-management challenges. Companies can assuage naysayers and stay current by agreeing to revisit standards every couple of years.

A good way to begin is to learn from what experts are doing. Seek out those highly regarded by peers and managers in your company's core quantitative areas—for instance, in finance, in marketing, or at the center of any product group whose product relies on analytics. One global financial services company took this approach and discovered that its top data scientists had settled on Python as a language. Even junior data scientists were sharing Python code through Jupyter Notebooks, a tool widely adopted in the scientific community for conducting and documenting reproducible research with code.

People who have spent years honing their applied quantitative skills will inevitably be opinionated when it comes to the choice of tools and methods and would most likely be delighted if their unofficial standards became official. These individuals can act as torchbearers and teachers in the organization, so raising their profiles and amplifying their impact is both sound business practice and a useful talent management strategy.

Create Shared-Code Repositories

Once people transcribe ideas in a common language, companies should take a cue from open-source communities and establish their own shared-code repositories and knowledge bases.

As with any central system, companies need to be thoughtful about security and permissions, and they should tailor access credentials according to their own standards for confidentiality or intellectual property protection. But creating a rich space where ideas can benefit from a wide array of contributions is a powerful way to promote learning and progress across organizational boundaries.

With shared-code repositories, multiple groups within an organization can use the same code files to solve similar problems. For instance, the marketing team in a bank might want to know about customers who are thinking about mortgage refinancing to target them for certain products; the finance team might also want data on possible refinancing as it projects budgets and billings. The problem formulation is the same in both cases—how many people, and which ones, are likely to refinance—so why not use the same code to get to the answer?

To get going quickly, pick a project, create a code repository around it, and invite contributions from a wide audience. Code-sharing platforms like GitHub and Bitbucket make this easy. It's useful to start with broadly applicable and noncontroversial projects—such as time-series forecasting, generating customer segmentations, and calculating price elasticities, to name a few.

Some organizations have gone beyond internal repositories and publicly shared their efforts. Leading technology companies like Google and Microsoft have been doing this for some time. But now, companies in other industries are also beginning to see the advantages of adopting this strategy. One telecom carrier, for example, has made its shared-code repositories part of the open-source community, which allows the company to avail itself of help from outsiders and potentially set the standard platform for the telecom industry.

Make Code Business as Usual

To generate the most value possible from advanced analytics, make code-based modeling the rule, not the exception. It should be as unremarkable and reflexive as attaching a spreadsheet to an email. This requires not just a change in perspective but also a change in habits.

You can accelerate this shift in your organization by communicating clear and specific expectations at all levels. You might, for instance, broadcast companywide messages emphasizing your focus on analytical excellence, explicitly connect it to company strategy in town hall-style meetings, and signal your

Code-based modeling should be as unremarkable and reflexive as attaching a spreadsheet to an email. This requires not just a change in perspective but also a change in habits.

intentions to shareholders and the market as a whole by high-lighting your efforts in everything from annual Securities and Exchange Commission filings to investor calls.

It's also critical to provide—and protect—time for employee training. Developing coding skills requires focus, feedback, elapsed time, and repetition. Whatever modes of instruction you choose—boot camps, massive open online courses (MOOCs), customized onsite workshops—trainees must have dedicated blocks of time to learn without constantly toggling back to their day jobs. Context switching slows down the process consider-ably. Becoming a competent coder takes focus.

Finally, you'll need to set up a viable support structure. Prog-ress stalls when everyone repeatedly goes to the same few super-users for help. Those individuals quickly become overwhelmed. Employees who are one step ahead in the journey can be tapped to mentor those who are just starting out. Few things provide a stronger incentive to learn something than knowing that you'll have to teach it to others.

2

Leisure Is Our Killer App

Adam Waytz

Depending on which forecasts you believe, we should be either moderately concerned[1] or extremely concerned[2] about robots taking our jobs in the near future. From truck drivers to lawyers to those designing the robots themselves, nobody is safe from being replaced by software, algorithms, and machines. Now that we are face-to-face (or face-to-screen) with that threat, an entire cottage industry has emerged around dispensing advice on how to prepare for it. Much of this advice centers on mastering skills that robots ostensibly cannot.

What skills are needed to avoid being automated out of a job? One article suggests the answer is all of them: "The more skills, knowledge, and experience you have, the less likely you are to be replaced or automated, so acquire whatever you can, as fast as you can."[3] But this "more is more" approach isn't sustainable, especially given the rapidly changing nature of work and the imperative to keep learning and adapting.

When recommending specific areas for development, management and technology experts tend to focus on two broad classes of skills that distinguish people from machines[4]—what

I'll refer to as *sociability* and *variability*. But homing in on those areas can still lead to burnout, leaving us even more vulnerable to obsolescence.

It's Exhausting to Be Human

Akin to social and emotional intelligence, sociability involves understanding others' emotions and seeing situations from alternative points of view, or what social psychologists call perspective-taking. It's a skill set that enables empathic collaboration with colleagues and customers, and many organizations are making it a priority for employee development. The retail pharmacy chain Walgreens, for example, launched an initiative for its pharmacists and beauty consultants to undergo empathy training to help cancer patients find products to manage treatment side effects such as hair loss, dry skin, and fatigue.[5]

The push for employees to master sociability—increasingly common now that *empathy* has become a corporate buzzword—may partly be a response to the rise of automation. In research I conducted with Harvard Business School marketing professor Michael Norton,[6] we found that people are particularly averse to robots taking jobs that require social and emotional skills (think social worker), but they are more comfortable with robots taking jobs that require analytical skills (think data analyst). Though the respondents were speaking for themselves, not for their employers, organizations seem inclined to divvy up work along similar lines.

Variability, the second skill set experts urge us to develop in the automation age, is our capacity for managing change and variety at work. Robots are extremely good at doing the same thing over and over, and so, we logically assume, humans should be more dynamic. What does variability look like in practice? It largely involves three things: detecting outliers, multitasking, and learning. Detecting outliers means responding to information that is rare or unexpected. People tend to do this more effectively than machines. Recently, for example, automaker Tesla attempted to fully automate its assembly line but discovered its robots could not manage "unexpected orientations of objects," which then required the attention of human workers.[7] Multitasking and learning, the other two manifestations of variability, are workplace skills we've been talking about for some time. In the current era, however, they've taken on greater urgency as pressure builds for employees to work faster and stay relevant.

Despite evidence that work involving sociability and variability can feel meaningful and motivating,[8] applying these skills nonstop is exhausting. Jobs that require high levels of sustained sociability—for instance, nursing and customer service—are some of the most susceptible to burnout and what psychologists call compassion fatigue, which can impair job performance and increase turnover. Jobs that require a great deal of variability—those for which people must continually shift between roles or tasks, develop new skills, or keep many things cooking at once—can be similarly draining, with negative consequences for job performance and turnover.[9]

Leisure as a Solution

Because sociability and variability, the qualities that set us apart from machines, are so taxing, leisure has become increasingly necessary for workers who fear being replaced by automation.

Those who feel threatened should *relax?* Yes, that's my argument, not because people are worry-free but because worrying tends to make matters worse, and leisure could actually give them an edge.

Some organizations are recognizing the importance of leisure for preventing burnout generally—forcing employees to take more vacation, giving them dedicated free time at work, turning off work email after hours, and my personal favorite, implementing an on-holiday autoreply to email, as Daimler has done.[10] To encourage employees to take real time off, the German automaker allows them to select an email setting that automatically deletes messages sent to them during vacation, lets senders know that the recipient will never see the messages, and encourages senders to email again after a specified date or to contact someone else. Programs like this one typically intend to reverse or prevent the negative effects of an always-on work culture. The 24/7 workplace simply keeps us plugged into our work, whereas the push toward sociability and variability makes that work more demanding. Leisure can mitigate the depleting effects from both sources.

The Benefits of a Wandering Mind

Beyond reducing employee burnout, however, leisure serves an additional function in the age of automation. Leisure itself is an activity that robots cannot perform, and it might actually make us better thinkers and workers.

When I visited the San Francisco Bay Area to interview people in the technology industry for my research on the psychological consequences of automation, I asked everyone I met the same question: "What is something a human can do that a robot cannot?" Henry Wang, a former venture capitalist associate who worked on investments in companies involved in artificial intelligence, gave my favorite answer: "A robot's mind cannot wander." Of course, this is supposed to be the advantage of robots, because it allows them to always stay on task. But this also means they cannot experience any of the benefits of mind-wandering, a state that occurs when we are at leisure.

Several lines of research suggest that mind-wandering is associated with specific cognitive benefits. One study showed that adults with attention deficit hyperactivity disorder, whose minds are prone to wandering off-task, perform better than non-ADHD adults in real-world creative pursuits, such as the visual arts, and score higher on a laboratory test of creative original thinking.[11] In other research, participants who twice took a simple creativity test (for instance, "How many unusual uses can you generate for a paper clip?") performed better the second time around if given a nondemanding activity such as a simple memory task to spur mind-wandering before retaking the test. They came up with ideas that were more unique.[12]

What explains these findings? Recent studies led by Dartmouth psychologist Meghan Meyer (and coauthored by me) suggest one possible answer.[13] We found that people who are highly successful in real-world creative pursuits and laboratory creative tasks are better at thinking beyond the here and now and show increased neural activity in brain regions involved in this type of thinking. In other words, highly creative people think more deeply about different points in time (the past and present), different places, and alternative realities. What does that have to do with the cognitive benefits of leisure? By encouraging our minds to wander, leisure activities pull us out of our present reality, which in turn can improve our ability to generate novel ideas or ways of thinking.

Again, this is something robots don't experience. You can turn a machine off and on to reboot it, but this simply simulates sleep. Leisure is more than that. When we let our minds drift away from work, we return to our tasks capable of tackling them in more inventive and creative ways. By prioritizing leisure, we can nurture and protect the qualities that set humans apart and improve work in the process.

3

Self-Reports Spur Self-Reflection

Angela Duckworth

"Know thyself."
—Socrates

I've been studying grit for 15 years, but the notion that some people stick with things much longer than others is not at all new. A century ago, Stanford psychologist Catherine Cox studied the lives of 301 eminent achievers. Cox concluded that the artists, scientists, and leaders who change the world have a striking tendency to hold fast to their goals and to work toward these far-off ambitions with dogged tenacity.

Picking up where Cox left off, I wanted to see whether grit—the combination of passion and perseverance toward long-term goals—would predict achievement in the 21st century. I was curious about how this aspect of our character relates to age, gender, and education. I wanted to unpack grit's motivational, behavioral, and cognitive underpinnings. In short, my aim was to study grit scientifically. To do so, I needed to measure it.

Why are scientists like me obsessed with measurement? In the immortal words of Lord Kelvin: "When you can measure what you are speaking about, and express it in numbers, you know

)ut it; but when you cannot measure it, when you
s it in numbers, your knowledge is of a meager
tory kind; it may be the beginning of knowledge,
but you have scarcely in your thoughts advanced to the stage of
science, whatever the matter may be."[1]

That is, a valid measure illuminates what you're trying to
understand, and understanding is the whole point of scientific
inquiry.

Questionnaires are one way to assess personal qualities like
grit. Performance tasks, informant ratings, biodata, and interviews are alternatives. But in psychological research, in part
because of their low cost and ease of administration, self-report
questionnaires are far more common.

The disadvantages of asking people to rate themselves are
obvious. You can, if you're motivated, fake your way to a higher
score. You may interpret the questionnaire items differently
than other people. You might hold yourself to higher (or lower)
standards. The list goes on.

But self-report questionnaires have unique advantages, too.
Nobody in the world but you—not your boss, your best friend,
or even your spouse—has 24/7 access to your thoughts, feelings,
and behavior. Nobody has more interest in the subject (you)
than yourself. And collecting data using questionnaires can be
incredibly efficient: In my experience, it takes about six seconds
for the average adult to read, reflect, and respond to a questionnaire item.

For those reasons, I decided to develop a self-report questionnaire for grit. I began by interviewing high achievers. I asked
these exceptional women and men, who had all garnered acco-
lades in their respective fields, how they had become successful.

And I inquired about their heroes and what they most admire about them.

Next, I distilled these observations into self-report statements that, whittled down to the 12 most reliable and valid, became the Grit Scale.[2] Further streamlining those to eight items, I then created the Short Grit Scale.[3] Perseverance was indexed, for example, by items like "I finish whatever I begin." Passion indicators were harder to develop, in part because when you ask people whether they have long-term goals, they tend to answer affirmatively. So instead, I wrote reverse-coded statements like "I have difficulty maintaining my focus on projects that take more than a few months to complete."

With this questionnaire, I discovered that grit predicts professional and academic success, particularly in domains that are both challenging and personally meaningful.[4] I found grit to be essentially unrelated to talent and intelligence. Instead, grit predicts how much you practice in order to improve. Grit scores increase with age and, perhaps relatedly, go hand in hand with the motivation to seek purpose and meaning in life, as opposed to pleasure.[5] As a scientist, I hadn't thought much about the effect that taking the Grit Scale might have on people. Then I met two visionary educators named Dave Levin and Dominic Randolph. Dave cofounded the KIPP charter school network, and Dominic is the head of school at Riverdale Country School.

Both educators were passionate about character development and wanted to help their students grasp what it means to exemplify character strengths like grit, gratitude, and curiosity. In their experience, talking about character in the abstract was fruitless because, well, exhortations like "Show some grit!" are utterly mysterious to a 13-year-old who can't read your mind.

Their intuition was that young people would benefit from knowing about qualities like grit in more granular detail. They believed that engaging in conversation—not just once but repeatedly—about specific thoughts, feelings, and behaviors exemplifying character would scaffold self-awareness and, in turn, growth. In sum, they believed that carefully crafted questionnaires might make that conversation easier to have by laying the foundations of a shared language of character development.

Together, Dave, Dominic, and I worked to develop a questionnaire that became known as the Character Growth Card. Unlike the original Grit Scale, items for grit and other character strengths were written with adolescents in mind and in fact were generated in collaboration with middle school students and their teachers.

After establishing that the Character Growth Card was reliable and valid both in its self-report version and as an informant rating form designed for teachers to assess their students, Dave and Dominic invited students and teachers in their schools to complete the questionnaire at the end of each marking period. Next, the item-level data was openly shared with each student, their teachers, and the students' parents. Unlike academic grades or standardized achievement test scores, there were no stakes: This information was not used to reward or punish "good" or "bad" behavior. Instead, openly discussing these observations was the whole point.

In his famous book *Last Lecture*, Carnegie Mellon University professor Randy Pausch said that "educators best serve students by helping them be more self-reflective."[6] And Dave and Dominic saw the questionnaire as a tool to do exactly that.

So did Anson Dorrance, a soccer coach I met a few years later.

Anson is the most decorated coach in women's soccer history and among the most celebrated coaches in any sport. His team, the University of North Carolina Tar Heels, has won a record 22 national championships. He coached the US women's national team to their first World Cup title and more recently racked up his record 1,000th career victory.

In our very first conversation, Anson told me he decided to give the Grit Scale to all 31 players on his team. I was surprised. In such a tiny sample, the questionnaire would not be precise enough for scientific research. Two beats later, I realized that Anson wouldn't be doing scientific research, anyway.

So why go to the trouble?

"I give it so that my players have a deeper appreciation for the critical qualities of successful people," Anson explained. "In some cases, the scale captures them, and in some cases, it *exposes* them."

Year after year, returning players take the Grit Scale again. Anson thinks that reading the Grit Scale questions and then reflecting on how they do or don't apply helps his players see how gritty they are now, relative to before. The questions don't automatically make anyone grittier, of course. But self-awareness, he reasons, is one step toward self-actualization.

Frankly, the idea that a questionnaire like the Grit Scale might be useful as a tool for self-reflection hadn't occurred to me until Dave and Dominic, and then Anson, suggested it. But in retrospect, the notion seems blindingly obvious.

After all, in my former career as a management consultant, I'd taken the Myers-Briggs Type Indicator (MBTI). Despite doubtful psychometric properties and limited predictive validity, human resources specialists recognize, respect, and administer the MBTI more than any other measure.[7] If you're reading this, there's a

There's a good chance that you've taken the MBTI — and taken its four-letter horoscope seriously.

good chance that you've taken the MBTI—and taken its four-letter horoscope seriously. (I am, for the record, an ENFP.)

Because the limitations of the MBTI have been so eloquently described elsewhere, I'll simply point out that millions of people might be wrong about the validity of its insights, but they aren't wrong about the need—urgent and sincere—for insight itself. We pay good money and invest precious time in the MBTI because we want to know ourselves better.

Do I know for sure whether self-report questionnaires indeed accomplish that purpose? Was it helpful to publish the Grit Scale in my book at the behest of my editor, who said, "Angela, trust me. People will want to take the scale. They want to learn something about themselves"?

There's indirect evidence that reflecting on the items in self-report personality questionnaires might catalyze self-awareness and personal development. We know, for example, that asking hypothetical questions about a specific behavior can bias us to engage in that behavior in the future.[8]

It is also well-established that self-monitoring, the intentional and consistent observation of your own behavior, supports self-control in domains as diverse as dieting, abstinence from drinking, and schoolwork.[9]

More recently, a handful of positive psychology intervention studies suggests that identifying and then being encouraged to develop your strengths may increase well-being.[10]

Although more research is needed, I am compelled by the possibility that questionnaires might deepen self-awareness of strengths like grit. I am intrigued by the possibility that questionnaires used in this way might contribute to shared language, common understanding, and, ultimately, a culture of character.

For a century, psychologists have been obsessed with measurement for the purpose of scientific research. For much longer, human beings have been concerned with self-awareness and self-development.

How gritty are you? As a scientist, I'd like to know. But perhaps you, too, are just as curious. And perhaps the same measures developed for research might help you know yourself a bit better. If self-awareness illuminates the path to self-development, a questionnaire is a good place to begin.

4

Career Management Isn't Just the Employee's Job

Matthew Bidwell and Federica De Stefano

Careers are much more complex than they used to be, even within organizations. Now that companies have replaced rigid hierarchies with flatter, more fluid team-based structures to promote agile ways of working, they have also made it much harder for employees to figure out what their next job should be, let alone the one after that. This challenge is also increasingly a concern for employers, who must—for the sake of engagement and retention—show high performers how they can progress within the organization.

During the past year, researchers on the Wharton People Analytics team talked with managers at 14 industry-leading companies and hosted two daylong meetings to explore how organizations are helping their people build better careers. Through those discussions, we identified a couple of key ways that companies are using analytics to tackle the challenge.

Forging Pathways in Fluid Environments

A common first step for companies that apply analytics to building careers is to use HR data to map out the paths that people have pursued in the past. Because conventional career ladders based on a hierarchical organization chart have essentially disappeared, companies are starting to analyze the myriad ways people have advanced to highlight different pathways employees might pursue. At its simplest, such career mapping uses historical data to show what prior incumbents of a given role have gone on to do, allowing people who are currently in that job to see a range of plausible options for their next career move. In other cases, companies identify the jobs that have fed a given role to show the variety of paths employees can take toward a position they covet. Either way, analytics is being used to uncover options for advancement and growth that are not defined by formal organization charts but instead emerge from the decentralized decisions of employees and hiring managers as they craft careers within the organization.

A more ambitious and forward-looking version of career mapping also incorporates data on the kinds of skills and competencies needed for each job, looking for overlaps in profiles across jobs. Although not every company has such data, and developing competency profiles for different jobs from scratch can be a long and costly process, this approach can potentially highlight which roles are more similar in their requirements than they appear. This method is particularly valuable in fast-changing fields, where the continual emergence of new jobs and the disappearance of older ones make it difficult to infer career paths from historical data.

For example, many of the skills required for an HR analytics role—such as experience with organizational data and reporting, analytical proficiency, and the ability to communicate with business partners—may also be found within an organization's pool of financial analysts. Identifying these overlaps helps create new career opportunities for people in both roles, providing them with unexpected paths for internal development and growth, and it establishes new sources of talent for their teams. For jobs that are hard to fill, this approach can streamline search efforts and generate significant savings for the organization. As an additional benefit, bringing skills into the career-mapping process can help managers give employees actionable advice about which skills they would need to develop to transition into their next roles.

Connecting With 'Passive' Internal Candidates

A number of organizations are also trying to be more proactive about finding "passive" internal candidates—people who would most likely be very good at certain jobs but may not know about those openings or may not have considered applying. Identifying those candidates involves developing analytic models to predict how well each of the current employees within the organization would fit the profile for a given role. Recruiters can then reach out to the best fits and solicit applications. Being able to identify internal candidates doesn't just hold down recruitment costs—evidence suggests that internal hires consistently outperform people brought in from the outside.[1] As a result, a number of established organizations have been exploring how to use analytics to better identify promising candidates within their ranks, and a suite of startups are developing products that could help companies matchmake between their jobs and their people.

Building the models themselves is analytically very simple, requiring only rudimentary statistical or machine learning capabilities. The bigger challenge for most organizations is building and maintaining the robust data about jobs and employees that those models draw on. Some companies have rigorous and up-to-date information on job requirements—but almost none have the information on employee skills needed to figure out a good match.

One way organizations are trying to solve this problem is by building an internal LinkedIn-like system in which people can post their profiles and increase their internal visibility. After all, LinkedIn has much better data on most people's skills than their employers currently possess. But early attempts to implement internal skill profiles have suffered from chicken-and-egg problems: Recruiters don't use the systems because the profiles are not completed, so people don't bother to complete the profiles.

Some employers are making updated skill profiles a mandatory part of the performance review process, which might help. Others are exploring creating skill profiles directly from people's work products. For example, IBM is scraping data from internal documents and workflow information to infer workers' skills before asking people to validate their profiles.[2] Both approaches seem promising, although it is too early to confirm their effectiveness. What is clear, though, is that as organizations take more interest in managing the careers of their employees, they will need to substantially improve the quality of the data they maintain on them.

Taking the Long View

Systems to map internal career paths and identify internal candidates tend to have a short-term focus: What job should somebody take next? Yet in many cases, employees' careers within an organization will extend well beyond that next job. It's important to also consider what kinds of career paths most often lead to longer-term success.

For instance, you might ask: In the end, is it better to allow people to deepen their expertise in a particular specialization or to foster broader skill sets by moving employees across functions? The analytics team at one financial company discovered that "broadening" moves early in a career slowed progression initially but eventually allowed people to rise higher in the organization. Such benefits of breadth are consistent with what we know about executive hiring, but it is not clear that varied careers are always a good idea.[3]

Understanding the trade-offs of a given move both short and long term—and communicating openly with employees about how things may play out over their careers—can help people see the benefits of building their career within the company, promoting loyalty, retention, and engagement. It can build relationships that are meant to last.

5

Can We Really Test People for Potential?

Reb Rebele

Have you ever taken an aptitude or work personality test? Maybe it was part of a job application, one of the many ways your prospective employer tried to figure out whether you were the right fit. Or perhaps you took it for a leadership development program, at an offsite team-building retreat, or as a quiz in a best-selling business book. Regardless of the circumstances, the hope was probably more or less the same: that a brief test would unlock deep insight into who you are and how you work, which in turn would lead you to a perfect-match job and heretofore unseen leaps in your productivity, people skills, and all-around potential.

How's that working out for you and your organization?

My guess is that results have been mixed at best. On the one hand, a good psychometric test can easily outperform a résumé scan and interview at predicting job performance and retention. The most recent review of a century's worth of research on selection methods, for example, found that tests of general mental ability (intelligence) are the best available predictors of job performance, especially when paired with an integrity test.[1]

Yet assessing candidates' and employees' potential presents significant challenges. We'll look at some of them here.

People Metrics Are Hard to Get Right

For all the promise these techniques hold, it's difficult to measure something as complex as a person for several reasons:

Not all assessments pass the sniff test. Multiple valid and reliable personality tests have been carefully calibrated to measure one or more character traits that predict important work and life outcomes. But other tests offer little more than what some scholars call "pseudo-profound bullshit"—the results sound inspiring and meaningful, but they bear little resemblance to any objective truth.[2]

People often differ more from themselves than they do from one another. Traditional psychological assessments are usually designed to help figure out whether people who are more or less *something* (fill in the blank: intelligent, extraverted, gritty, what have you), on average, do better on whatever outcomes the organization or researcher is most interested in. In other words, they're meant to capture differences among people. But several studies have found that, during a two-week period, there can be even more variation within one individual's personality than there is from person to person.[3] As one study put it, "The typical individual regularly and routinely manifested nearly all levels of nearly all traits in his or her everyday behavior."[4] Between-person differences can be significant and meaningful, but within-person variation is underappreciated.

Many personality tests provide valid measures of traits that predict important outcomes. Countless others offer results that sound meaningful but bear little resemblance to any objective truth.

People change – and not always when you expect them to. The allure of aptitude, intelligence, and personality tests is that they purport to tell us something stable and enduring about who people are and what they are capable of. Test makers (usually) go to great lengths to make sure people who take the test more than once get about the same score the second time around. Yet compelling evidence suggests that we can learn how to learn, sometimes in ways we didn't anticipate.[5] We can also shift our personalities in one direction or another (at least to some degree, though not always without cost) for both near-term benefits and longer-term goals. Interestingly, one recent study with more than 13,000 participants found that people tend to become more conscientious right *before* getting a new job, which is conveniently around the time a hiring manager would be trying to figure out how hard they would work if they landed the role.[6]

The nature of the task can matter more than the nature of the person. Most of us have heard the theory that we each have a preferred learning style, and the more we can use the one that fits, the more we'll remember. Unfortunately, virtually no evidence supports that theory. That doesn't mean that all approaches to studying are equally effective—it's just that the strategy that works best often depends more on the task than on the person. Similarly, different parts of our personalities can serve different types of goals. We act extraverted when we want to connect with others or seize an opportunity, and we become disciplined when we want to get something done or avoid mistakes. In one study, conscientiousness especially emerged when the things that needed to get done were difficult and urgent— even for people who were not especially organized and hardworking in general.[7]

One way to read this list of challenges is to come away convinced that people analytics is a fool's errand. But that would ignore the fact that each of these caveats has been uncovered through rigorous analysis of people data.

Instead, it's probably more constructive to remember what personality psychologist Brian Little, while channeling psychologist Henry Murray and anthropologist Clyde Kluckhohn, says in his popular TED Talk: "Each of us is . . . in certain respects, like all other people, like some other people, and like no other person."[8] People analytics, in other words, needs to include better *person* analytics.

What It Would Take to Go Granular

What would better person analytics look like?

For starters, we would consider the context. Companies selling off-the-shelf assessments often tout the many thousands of diverse professionals who have already taken their survey to prove that it can work for all kinds of people and circumstances. A large validation effort can be a sign of an invaluable general-purpose tool, but that doesn't mean it's right for every job. Sometimes the situation calls for customization.

Consider a project that the Wharton People Analytics research team did with Global Health Corps (GHC), a leadership development organization aimed at improving health equity. Each year, GHC screens thousands of applications to find the most promising candidates for yearlong fellowships, and the management team had developed a hunch that a certain personality trait might be predictive of a fellow's job performance. So we devised multiple methods to measure it. The first was a general measure of said trait that was previously developed, validated, and published in a peer-reviewed journal, while the second was a new situational judgment test (SJT) we developed with GHC so that we could look for evidence of this trait in how people responded to a number of job-relevant scenarios. We also tried a more advanced linguistic analysis to flag indicators of this trait in candidates' application essays. Whereas the established measure had the best evidence behind it, and the linguistic analysis was the most technically sophisticated, in the end the situational judgment test was the only significant predictor of job performance for candidates.

When considering *why* this worked best, we think it's not just because the SJT took the organization's unique context into account but also because it captured the extent to which this trait showed up in many different situations, not just on average. Custom measures are not always the answer, but sometimes the context really is important.

Next, we would design new measures with variability in mind. Given the findings mentioned above about how much people's behavior can change from one situation to the next, it might seem paradoxical to even try to find something enduring about a person's character. But just because personality is dynamic does not mean it is undiscoverable. Some researchers have proposed using if-then questionnaires to detect nuanced patterns in each person's personality profile, although such techniques have yet to be well tested in the workplace.[9] A better approach might be to take repeated measures from the same employees over time. That is often easier said than done, given the challenges many organizations face in getting employees to fill out even a single survey. If the participation problem can be overcome, however, repeated measures can lead to insights—about what people are like in general and the ways in which they vary—that one-time surveys simply can't generate.

Earlier this year, for example, George Mason University researcher Jennifer Green and her colleagues took a novel approach to understanding the relationship between employees' personalities and their organizational citizenship behaviors (those often-underappreciated extra ways that employees support their colleagues and organizations over and above their job duties). By using an experience sampling methodology in which they collected multiple reports from more than 150 employees over the course of 10 workdays, they were able to show that employees with more consistent personalities were, in turn, more consistent in going beyond the call of duty—even after controlling for their general dispositions. For jobs where consistency is key to success, these researchers argued, repeated measures offer a chance to find stability in the variability of employees' personalities.[10]

Finally, we would give people their own data in ways that would help them develop. Although most employees won't have the skills or even the interest to track and analyze their own data, that doesn't mean they wouldn't be able to use it if it were summarized well and presented clearly.

Some tools have been designed expressly for that purpose. Microsoft MyAnalytics, for example, is an add-on to Office 365 that aims to reduce the pain of collaborative overload by sending you reports about your schedule and communication patterns. While there are nudges and recommendations built in, the basic premise behind the service is that providing you with a summary of your own data will help you identify your own strategies for making your work life better. In a similar vein, Ambit Analytics received a preseed round of funding in early 2018 for its technology that uses real-time voice analysis to coach managers in the moment on their communication skills. While the long-term viability and utility of both of these tools remains to be seen, both point to the potential for giving individuals more opportunities to learn from their own data.

Taking a more granular approach to people analytics does have its risks, of course. For one thing, because individuals can be more easily identified by their data, privacy may be an even larger worry than it normally is. It's a valid concern—one that underscores the need for vigilance. Organizations must develop robust policies and practices to govern ethical data collection, access, and use. They must also be transparent with employees not only about what kinds of data are being collected but also about what the data says about them. Open and ongoing dialogues about the costs and benefits of more personalized analytics should be as common as the legalese-filled privacy statements people too often just click through.

A bigger-picture concern is the risk of hypercustomization. Organizations are prone to an often-inaccurate uniqueness bias in which they assume that no other group of workers has ever been quite like them. That can lead to situations like the one I found myself in a few years ago, when senior leaders from two organizations independently—in the same week—asked me about the idea of measuring their employees' levels of grit. When I explained that grit is usually measured as passion and perseverance for long-term goals, both were quick to say that they were defining it differently for their context. One said it was really about resilience and tenacity at her nonprofit; the other insisted that ambition was at its core. They may each have identified important traits for their respective organizations, but the problem was that they both contended they wanted to measure something called "grit." If bespoke measurements with identical names start to proliferate, it'll become much harder for all of us to talk with and learn from one another.

And learning, after all, is the raison d'être for people analytics. Organizations invest in it because they hope it will tell them something about their current or future employees that will increase the odds of forming productive long-term relationships with them. Employees engage with it when they have a reasonable expectation that it might reveal something about themselves and who they might yet become in their careers. Both of these goals will be better served if we pursue a finer-grained understanding of human potential.

6

Does AI-Flavored Feedback Require a Human Touch?

Michael Schrage

Digital tools and technologies are now relentlessly and remorselessly transforming how performance management works. Customized and continuous data-driven feedback is becoming the new normal for enterprises worldwide. This feedback appears both qualitatively and quantitatively superior to its performance review precursors and should lead to better outcomes. But does AI-flavored feedback require a human touch to measurably improve its impact?

Organizations committed to state-of-the-art talent management are revisiting the role managers should play in delivering, facilitating, and/or curating employee feedback. Are managers mainly conduits for criticism? Or do they add meaningful value and insight? "We know that putting the manager back in performance management is one of the keys to making it work," said McKinsey & Company partner Bryan Hancock during a recent webinar on performance management.[1] "You can create the best system in the world with the best amount of employee involvement," he said, "but if at key junctures, the managers aren't taking responsibility, it's a problem"—especially since Netflix,

Google, Amazon, and other digital innovators have successfully personalized sophisticated analytic assessments for their users.

Whether or not average managers represent an organization's best option for constructively critiquing employees is now an open and important question. Preliminary findings from our recent research suggest that ongoing investment and innovation in AI capabilities will provoke conflicting answers. The implications for legacy HR and people management are enormous.

This research highlights how direct managerial involvement both complements and competes with data-determined performance reviews. Increasingly, organizations are discovering they must explicitly choose whether humans or machines should get the last word on people's performance. This process is as much about cultural transformation as organizational transition. However, productively balancing analytic insight with managerial interaction is challenging. Who owns the feedback?

IBM's digital journey offers a superb case study in confronting these performance management challenges. The company's HR leadership, for example, explicitly tracks managerial impact on employee engagement and outcomes.

"The role of the manager is incredibly important still, even in an agile culture," acknowledges Diane Gherson, IBM's chief human resources officer and senior vice president of human resources. "If there's a manager who's not 'bought in' or not engaged, the chances of their people not being engaged is something like three times higher. Making sure that managers fully understand the strategy and are fully engaged really can't be forgotten."

But Gherson emphasizes that her group's intensifying commitment to AI has dramatically changed IBM's human capital management. "We've got a lot of AI in our HR," she notes. That investment profoundly alters how managers and employees engage with one another. Smarter software has fundamentally restructured IBM's performance management economics and expectations. Increased digitalization often disintermediates direct managerial engagement.

AI's most significant influence is on productivity, says Gherson. HR has replaced many human resources with chatbots, for example, that learn to advise employees while generating analytics for monitoring how helpful the advice proves to be. In other words, IBM gets feedback on feedback.

Comparable AI systems offer decision support with actionable insights into possible attrition and suggestions about appropriate pay levels for employees with highly competitive skill sets. "Enabling better employee experiences" is another AI focus, Gherson says. These systems embrace career development advice, personalized learning programs, and Blue Matching (IBM's proprietary system that intelligently matches candidates to desirable job openings within the company).

As important as managers may be, IBM HR's clarion message is that digitalization must deliver smarter, better, faster, and more engaging talent management services for less. Personalized and productive feedback can't come at a premium price. At the same time, most organizations authentically want their higher-cost human managers engaged and involved.

This conflicted sensibility and expectation is not unique. ADP vice president and chief behavioral economist Jordan Birnbaum observes that empowering managers and employees has become an important part of performance management systems design. "When performance management is designed well," he says, "managers have a toolbox that helps them improve by several orders of magnitude, leaving employees feeling empowered to succeed moving forward."

The catch, he acknowledges, is that being objectively data-driven often forces people to incorporate uncomfortable algorithmic advice. "If you're going to use evaluative data properly," says Birnbaum, "then the job is to frame that data properly, particularly if it is being used to drive future performance. That also includes incorporating feedback not easily measurable or captured by data, like *teamwork* or *supportiveness*. But as long as relevant data is not easily captured, there's a place for the human manager in the process. Whether the human manager feels that to be the case, though, is another story."

The tension becomes obvious: Is being asked—or told—to follow a prescription that makes one measurably better a source of managerial empowerment or disempowerment? For managers and employees alike, does it bring about more confusion? For example, would managers have the discretion to ignore or significantly alter their data-driven advisories? How do conflicts between intuition and evidence get resolved? Most managers are grateful for contextually relevant analytic advice. But advice that must be followed is no longer advice—it's compulsion.

As AI and machine learning technologies improve, says Birnbaum, managerial prescriptions become even more specific and explicit. This leads to a natural question: At what point does it make sense—and save money—to simply bypass the manager as a feedback delivery system and directly advise the employee?

7

What Managers Can Gain from Anonymous Chats

Ryan Bonnici

Anonymous chat apps are quickly picking up steam in the workplace, providing employees with a platform to discuss concerns and complaints, offer advice, and provide unfiltered feedback in novel ways. These technologies can be helpful to managers—but you wouldn't think so from much of the press surrounding them.

Blind, one of the most popular of these apps and dubbed "HR's worst nightmare" by TechCrunch, offers employees the opportunity to provide raw feedback, which is "the antithesis to HR's utopic vision of a manageable and orderly corporate culture."[1] The *New York Times* has looked at the trouble anonymous feedback gives employees and managers, citing expert research that anonymous peer reviews are just as political and subjective as any others. Contently cofounder Shane Snow announced in January 2018 that his company was ending most anonymous employee feedback, which had opened a platform for snide, nonconstructive remarks that left the team "with little but hurt feelings."[2]

These are all valid concerns. But as a manager myself, I've found that there is a time and place for collecting anonymous feedback from my staff. In fact, doing so can help retain great employees, boost productivity, and build greater engagement.

To be clear, it is important to have a workplace culture based on real, open communication and transparency so employees feel free to share their concerns and ideas by name without fear of reprisal. Far too many companies are failing to build these cultures. In fact, according to a study by *MIT Sloan Management Review* and Deloitte on digital leadership, "C-level executives often portray their organizations as transparent, open to risk-taking, and having high morale. But as you move down the organizational structure, managers rarely believe it and say that the level of trust is very low."[3]

It's clearly important to address this at the manager level. It's why I meet with every person on my team—not just my direct reports, but with their reports as well, at least once a month. I work to build relationships with them and encourage them to bring me anything that they feel deserves my attention. When they do, I try to help them and follow up, as building trust is crucial for fostering environments where feedback can be shared openly.

Still, I know that, even with this culture in place, there may be things that some employees just aren't comfortable sharing by name—particularly when it concerns their team or their immediate manager.

For gathering anonymous workplace feedback, I use an employee engagement tool called TINYpulse. At least once a month, I send out this question to my entire team and its reporting chain: On a scale of 1 to 10, how happy are you with your job?

We generally get about an 80% response rate. And most replies are good news, with people reporting high numbers. But sometimes an employee responds with a low number. When that happens, I can use the tool to create an anonymous dialogue with that individual. I respond in an authentic, transparent way, writing something like, "Hey, this is Ryan. I'm really sorry to learn that you're feeling this way. Could you help me understand better, so I can help drive changes for you?"

For example, one employee recently reported being at a 5 on the survey. After I reached out, this person explained that the problem was about feeling unappreciated. So I asked them to explain a bit more: Does this feeling relate to your manager? To the team in general? Or is this within another team? It led to a longer conversation, as these types of communications almost always do.

About half the time, the person ends up choosing to share his or her identity and gives details that help me address the concern more specifically. I maintain their confidentiality and keep an eye out for the problem—how this person is treated in meetings, for example, or whether their work is being recognized by his or her manager and by the company in general.

Even when people choose not to identify themselves, it's still helpful for me to learn at least the general nature of what's making them feel less satisfied. It perks up my eyes and ears, so I become more attuned to that kind of problem festering anywhere in the organization.

So, unlike with chat boards, I'm not creating an open platform for people to make any and all complaints anonymously. It isn't a tool for people to trash-talk each other or to post nebulous remarks that don't lead anywhere. Managers can see anonymous results of the survey in aggregate, and anyone can reach out anonymously to anyone else, offering the chance to talk. But any responses are private, one-to-one.

I've found that it consistently enhances, rather than diminishes, our culture of open communication. It also sends a message: Our employees are so important to us, we will use every tool we can to help address problems.

It's difficult to overestimate the importance of employee satisfaction. Research has shown that higher levels of employee engagement can lead to higher profitability and that "when employees are satisfied, they tend to be more committed to their work and have less absenteeism, which positively influences the quality of the goods they produce and services they deliver."[4] Anonymous surveys looking at employee satisfaction can also help managers gauge their staff's willingness to serve as brand ambassadors.

As employees find new ways to use digital tools to share stories, offer advice, or even simply let off steam, it won't be feasible for employers to avoid anonymous technologies altogether. Instead, managers must look for ways to use them effectively—by making them part of an ecosystem that values relationships, open communication, and employee feedback in all its forms.

8

Are Your Employees Driven to Digital Distraction?

Brian Solis

As an analyst and adviser to tech companies, I've long known the tricks that digital platforms use to get people addicted. I didn't think it would happen to me. But a few years ago, I fell into the trap.

Throughout the day, I could barely go a few minutes without checking notifications on my phone. My productivity suffered, as did my relationships and life outside of work.

The digital distraction trap happens in businesses across all industries and affects workers of all age groups. It's taking a toll on worker well-being. A 2012 study estimated that digital distractions cost businesses more than $10,000 per worker per year. According to a more recent report from Udemy, nearly two-thirds of workers (62%) spend about an hour of each workday looking at their phones.[1]

The survey found that most employers are lagging when it comes to helping employees "manage the constant barrage of noise, interruptions, and notifications in order to maintain performance." Seventy percent of workers say training would help people block out distractions. But 66% have not spoken to their managers about the need for this training, "perhaps because they feel insecure about revealing areas of perceived weakness."

If you want your employees to regain their focus, here are four steps you can take as a manager. I recommend them in the spirit of sharing what's helped me and others.

Teach the Pomodoro Technique. Starting off with strict rules such as "no looking at your phones for the next hour" won't do much for long-term improvement and may build resentment rather than engagement on teams. We've been trained like Pavlov's dog to respond to our notifications and even anticipate them. Often, we don't even realize we're doing it.

The key is for us to unlearn this response, so we can start letting those impulses go.

One way to do that and make better use of uninterrupted periods of time is to use the Pomodoro Technique. The goal is to focus on a single task for 25 minutes, followed by a break of about five minutes. Since you know that a break is coming, it's easier to resist the urge to check each notification that pops up or become distracted by nonwork-related tasks.

Some people may adapt more quickly to these time-blocked efforts than others. I had to start with much shorter blocks of time, working my way up to 25 minutes. Challenge your employees to do the same. Offer them a space to store their devices out of reach. Encourage them to check out apps that show them how often they pick up their phones throughout the day.

If you receive pushback, lead with empathy. Emphasize that you're in it together—after all, we've been conditioned by technology in recent years. With this approach, individuals and teams can get more work done by focusing for set periods of time. You can also offer to tell other departments and even clients that "this is how we work now," so that they can expect email replies within two hours rather than two minutes. In the end, this will be a better way of working for all parties.

Turn the clock back on open offices. While the post-dot-com era has seen an explosion of open office plans, with many organizations literally breaking down office and cubicle walls to create more open spaces, recent research conducted at Harvard Business School has found that open office plans can actually be highly detrimental to productivity and collaboration.

While it's good for offices to include open areas in which people can talk and collaborate, it's also important to give workers their own spaces away from all the noise. In fact, in Udemy's survey, workers cited chatty colleagues and office noise as even bigger problems than digital distractions.

But even digital distractions are made worse by open offices. You can turn off your own phone, but it won't stop you from hearing all the beeping and buzzing of everyone else's devices from across the room. And hearing those notifications can add to the temptation to abandon the work at hand and check your own.

When possible, I encourage managers to provide people with offices (whether they're individual offices or shared quiet rooms). The ability to close a door makes a big difference. And providing employees with noise-canceling headphones is also a great solution—not only because they can block out sounds, but also because they send a physical reminder to others not to interrupt colleagues when they're doing focused work.

Establish a plan for urgent situations. Even if people manage to reduce tech addiction and work in quiet conditions, they still often rightfully feel the need to check every digital notification just in case it's urgent.

I recommend that managers set up a protocol exclusively for urgent messages—and use it sparingly. This could be a tool that emits a special sound when something is marked as urgent.

Digital distractions are made worse by open offices. You can turn off your own phone, but it won't stop you from hearing all the beeping and buzzing of everyone else's devices from across the room.

An easy-to-use setting on computers, phones, and tablets can block out all other notifications, allowing only urgent messages through. I also suggest making it possible for anyone in the organization to mark an email as urgent, rather than having all emails from certain senders (such as your boss) show up as urgent.

And when people are on vacation, don't expect them to see email at all. If they absolutely must be contacted in an emergency, text or call them.

Model best behaviors. Ultimately, one of the most powerful things we can do as managers to fix distracted working conditions and restore productivity is to engage in the right behaviors ourselves.

During staff meetings, those of us in leadership positions should make it standard practice to avoid looking at our emails, Slack messages, or anything else on our phones. When we chat with employees, we should not assume they've already seen nonurgent emails that we sent them in just the previous hour. And when we're sitting (or standing) at our desks, employees should see us focusing, uninterrupted, for substantial periods of time.

It isn't easy. Accomplishing all this means going against the grain of how our offices have evolved in recent years. But I know from experience that when we take these steps, our work lives become better—and our businesses more successful.

II

Managing Teams

9

Get Things Done with Smaller Teams

Chris DeBrusk

An important executive goal in most large companies is to improve efficiency and effectiveness. With top-line revenue growth elusive in most markets, a key way to increase returns to shareholders is to boost the bottom line—and that means stepping up productivity. These gains need to come from improving the processes that *run* the company as well as those that *change* it.

Unfortunately, achieving greater productivity in project teams focused on change can be challenging, especially when new technology is involved. Every company has experienced a project that was either delivered at twice the budget and in double the time, or never actually delivered against its objectives and eventually scrapped. There are many reasons why these large programs fail, but one potential root cause is that they simply break down under their own weight. One way to improve the effectiveness of projects is to reduce the size of the teams mobilized to tackle them. In other words, it might be time to make your project teams smaller.

Smaller teams move faster, iterate at a higher frequency, and innovate more for the company. There are endless examples of small teams achieving amazing things. When Facebook purchased WhatsApp for $19 billion, the company's 32 engineers had created a platform that was used by 450 million users. The Volkswagen Golf GTI, one of the most famous hot hatchbacks in history, was created by a team of eight. Many of the largest technology companies created their first successful products with teams of fewer than 10 people.

Jeff Bezos famously instituted a "two-pizza rule" in the early days of Amazon. His edict was that any team that could not be fed by two pizzas was too big. In concept, it is fairly easy to understand how a smaller team can be more effective, as communication is easier and decision making can be accomplished more quickly.

But practically, how can managers take advantage of this technique in large organizations?

Make Big Problems Smaller Problems

Establishing two-pizza teams is especially challenging with in-flight programs in large organizations that tend to grow over time. If you track the scope of a major change initiative, you'll often find that by the end of the project, the goals of the program bear little resemblance to those that were agreed on at the beginning. This growth effect is vastly multiplied as the size of the program and the team supporting it grows. New team members bring new goals that have to be incorporated into the program (and, of course, nothing is ever removed).

One way to control this natural program weight gain is to break down the project from the beginning into discrete problems that can be solved by smaller teams. With leadership focus, even large, complex problems can be compartmentalized into separate, achievable pieces that a small team can easily take on and over-deliver.

Another way to get smaller without actually shrinking your organization is to break business capabilities into focused organizational units, each with a clear mandate to provide the company with a discrete set of services that are well-defined and understood. Then put someone in charge and give them responsibility and authority to get things done—and see what they can accomplish.

Ensure No Team Member Is Indispensable

One of the realities of many large organizations is that few people have the luxury of working only on a single problem. As problems and the teams that aim to solve them multiply, key people get split across many competing tasks, so their time is sliced into small, difficult-to-manage increments. When a critical member of a team is simultaneously working as a member of six other teams, delivery against critical milestones is inevitably affected. Just getting on that person's calendar becomes difficult.

It is important to actively manage away from "indispensable" people in your change and transformation projects. Single-threading important decisions to any one person creates a single point of failure for the team. As a result, projects and innovations move at a slower pace and operate with higher risk. Small teams allow you to take steps more easily to cross-train as a way to manage this risk.

Adopt One-Step Decisions

Large teams are notorious for needing multiple steps to make most decisions. Aligning calendars often takes time, and once you get everyone into a room (or, more likely, on a call), several attendees need to be brought up to speed. Some attendees will not have read the requisite material, and others will have been sent as substitutes for key decision-makers who could not make the time (and these substitutes will not be able to make any critical decisions without conferring with their boss). We've all attended these sorts of meetings. They rarely result in decisions—and they usually lead to additional meetings. A small team can shortcut these issues much more easily. Fewer people need to be present to make decisions, and those present are typically much more involved in the details of the problem, so they don't need a meeting to ramp up before they can contribute.

When you first form a team, spend time to determine what types of decisions each member of the team can make on their own, what types of decisions the team can make as a group, and what needs to be escalated for more senior input. Then fight hard to push as much of the decision making to the team by defining very clear guidelines that give the team ownership and accountability.

Build Trust

There is nothing more powerful in a team than trust. It accelerates progress, improves quality, and reduces execution risk. Yet trust doesn't come automatically and often needs to be intentionally created. Smaller teams allow managers to spend more time with each person, getting to know their strengths, weaknesses, and career goals. They can structure tasks in a way that reinforces the natural strengths of the team, which allows team members to show their competence, and that builds trust. Team members also build trust through constant interactions as they tackle and solve problems together.

A successful team event outside of work doesn't hurt, either. Sometimes trust is built in the bowling alley, the paintball pitch, the basketball court, or just enjoying good food.

Be Less Formal When Sharing Information

Presentations are an amazing tool for communicating complex ideas. They are also a huge time sink for teams. By moving to smaller, more focused teams, you can reduce, if not eliminate, the need for the structured communication that a presentation provides.

A small, focused team can easily replace a formal presentation and slide deck that requires hours to create with a whiteboard session where the problem and solution are diagrammed out in real time. If the team is not colocated, there are many collaboration tools like Slack, Microsoft Teams, and Symphony that can replace a physical whiteboard and move the brainstorming online. The impact is the same: faster solutions and greater alignment across the team.

Increase Visibility (and Accountability)

It is fairly easy to hide in a large team. You can dial into conference calls and avoid contributing. Since deliverables are owned by multiple people, it is easy to let others do the heavy lifting. You can be busy during key meetings where you need to be prepared. We've all worked on teams in which no one really knew what some members were doing.

With small teams, hiding is nearly impossible. A lack of contribution is immediately noticed, and those who don't contribute to moving the ball forward can be moved off the team much

more easily because there is direct evidence that they are not
adding value.

Limit Unnecessary Synchronous Meetings

While it clearly isn't possible to eliminate conference calls
entirely, the ubiquitousness of collaboration platforms like
Slack, instant messaging, and desktop videoconferencing means
that teams can communicate in many ways that don't revolve
around conference calls, with all of their inherent challenges.

Small teams can avoid conference calls because they communicate often, through multiple channels, both digital and face-
to-face. Large teams don't interact nearly as much and therefore
need regular catch-ups to re-sync on objectives and ensure information is being shared effectively. Even then, conference calls
are still relatively ineffective in ensuring alignment.

Focus Less on Tracking Project Progress

Project managers live to track things. They make lists of tasks
and track progress against them. They identify dependencies
and track relative slippage. An effective project manager is able
to act like oil for a large project team, reducing friction just when
it threatens to affect delivery. Yet less effective project managers
spend their days bothering teams for status updates and creating
presentations aggregating the updates they received.

With the widespread adoption of tools like Slack and Jira,
the need for someone to play the role of progress aggregator is
quickly coming to an end because the platforms automate tracking. This is even more pronounced with smaller teams, who
communicate at such high bandwidth that everyone knows

what tasks are behind and what needs to be done to get them back on track.

Product managers are critical, but the usefulness of *project* managers should be questioned, especially as teams get smaller and more focused.

Work More Easily with Other Teams

As you break down programs into chunks that smaller teams can tackle, the interface between teams dependent on each other becomes critical. It is often friction between teams that turns into missed dependencies and timeline slippage.

It is important to craft "contracts" between teams that clearly outline their individual mandates, spell out how they will interact, and identify what they can rely on each other to provide and when. A focus on clear and concise dependency management increases transparency while ensuring that each team can focus on achieving the specific goals it has been assigned.

Embrace Technology Faster and More Effectively

Smaller, empowered business teams who have control of their own destiny start to figure out how to leverage technology to improve the world they now control more quickly—especially if you give them more direct oversight of the technology teams that support them.

In order to accomplish this, companies need to figure out which aspects of their technology delivery capability need to be centralized and which aspects can be decentralized and moved closer to the teams who are executing for customers and colleagues. Improvements also need to be made in the process of evaluating and approving the use of innovative technologies, as this is often a point of friction in larger organizations.

The emergence of machine learning as a critical business tool is an example that shows how technology teams are working to put sophisticated analytics capability into the hands of small teams of business users. While difficult to accomplish, a properly balanced technology delivery capability that supports execution teams will result in increased innovation and acceleration in meeting business goals.

As technology gets more modular and flexible and as organizations adopt agile delivery techniques, the concepts outlined above are likely to become more mainstream. If you want to reduce execution risk, increase the pace of innovation, and deliver faster, turn your big project into a group of smaller projects and let the teams get to work.

10

Why Teams Still Need Leaders

Lindred Greer, interviewed by Frieda Klotz

In recent years, agile and flat working structures have gained favor at many companies and struck a responsive chord with employees who are put off by stifling hierarchies. But doing away with hierarchy can cause confusion, spark complaints from employees, and hasten departures, says Lindred (Lindy) Greer, associate professor of management and organizations at the University of Michigan's Ross School of Business and faculty director at its Sanger Leadership Center. While agreeing that rigid forms of hierarchy can impede innovation, she has found that it can provide many important benefits when managed well.

Greer first became interested in team structures more than a decade ago while investigating diversity, hoping to understand how gender and race play out in social interactions. She found that team members tended to be less focused on their colleagues' gender and ethnicity than on the power they wielded. She then decided to explore how hierarchies work in organizations and what happens when they go wrong. She has written a number of groundbreaking articles on hierarchy, status, and the social dynamics of teams, including, most recently, "Why and When Hierarchy Impacts Team Effectiveness" in the *Journal of Applied Psychology*.[1]

MIT Sloan Management Review correspondent Frieda Klotz spoke to Greer as she was preparing to travel to Seattle to coteach a course on leadership development with an orchestra conductor at a business incubator. What follows is an edited version of their conversation.

MIT Sloan Management Review: **A few years ago, many management experts and business leaders were saying that hierarchy had had its day and that the future belonged to flat organizations. What's happening? Is the pendulum swinging back?**

Greer: Hierarchy is probably the most common form of organizing the workplace. There aren't a lot of good alternatives to it, and companies need some say in managing workers, particularly as they scale. However, there are also a lot of downsides to hierarchy, and over the last decade my collaborators and I have documented the many ways in which it can go wrong. Team members squabble over resources, engage in power struggles, and battle over rank. All of this harms performance. One of the burning questions in management research right now is, what are the best alternatives to hierarchy? But it's a complex picture—hierarchy isn't always bad or harmful, and its effectiveness may depend on where and how it's implemented, and how the person at the top manages the hierarchy. For example, there is growing interest in remote work and virtual teams, and in that context, hierarchy works quite well.

Why is hierarchy a good way to structure virtual teams?

Hierarchy makes it easier to coordinate how people work together. So for teams that most need structure—those operating under uncertain conditions or when the task is unclear, as often happens in virtual or remote teams—hierarchy is highly effective. It still has downsides, but the need for it is so great that it trumps whatever internal politics and bureaucracy come with it. You simply need that structure to keep people moving together.

Often when people work remotely, there is an assumption that they have more autonomy and freedom than office workers do. But is it wrong to think so?

Hierarchy does not have to mean less autonomy. For example, when I talk to the CEOs of companies doing really well with a remote-work model—I'm thinking about Automattic, which owns WordPress, or 10up, a successful web design company— they emphasize the need for structure. In practice, this means that they put much more effort into coordinating how people work together than other companies. They formalize role descriptions and onboarding better, and they're more intentional and specific in their recruiting and hiring. For example, they'll do interviews through Slack to test independence and communication virtually. They say this makes them better at navigating the people side of business largely because the remote workforce is utterly intentional about the way interactions are structured.

But even though the workers are accountable to someone, they can still retain decision control in their areas of expertise because the company has clear values that guide how to make decisions. That's the thing: Hierarchy can go hand in hand with autonomy. It doesn't have to be one or the other.

What does your recent research say about how hierarchy works or doesn't work in an office environment?

Research has generally historically focused on the benefits of hierarchy. The core assumption, drawn from animal behavior, was that hierarchy was a natural way to organize people—that if one person was dominant, others would be more submissive. The research assumes that people find hierarchy comfortable and seek it out in times of crisis. My research challenges the view that hierarchy is always good by showing that it can lead to inequities and conflicts within teams. One of the problems is that the structure it provides isn't always the right one, in both the form of structure and the context in which it is applied. For example, people aren't always happy about how they're ranked, and there can be power struggles and turmoil around roles. In some contexts, like creative brainstorming, hierarchy just gets in the way and fosters competition rather than collaboration.

How does that kind of conflict affect team performance?

In the 2018 paper in the *Journal of Applied Psychology,* my co-authors and I showed that on average, hierarchy causes power struggles and personal conflicts and can thereby undermine team performance. In other research, we found that 70% of the time peer disputes turned into personal conflicts and power struggles.[2] This was really bad for the teams' productivity as well as for the employees' happiness.

Given the potential problems, what can companies do?

Managers need to be smarter about how they use hierarchy. Good leaders know how to flex—to use hierarchy to get things done but also to flatten the organization when they want workers to be creative. The Navy SEALs have an excellent approach: When they're on the ground, there's a clear chain of command. If their commander says, "Get out now," there's no playing devil's advocate—no one argues. You listen and you fall into rank.

But once they go back to the base to debrief, Navy SEALs literally take their stripes off at the door. When they sit down, ev-

"The Navy SEALs have an excellent approach: When they're on the ground, there's a clear chain of command. . . . But when they sit down [to debrief], everybody's equal and has a voice."

erybody's equal and has a voice. This is important because one person on the team might have noticed something really critical that nobody else saw, which could inform their plans for the next assignment. So they flatten out; they share ideas. Then they go back outside, put on their stripes and uniforms, and literally fall into rank again.

I spent the last half year or so studying startups to see if there were companies that had effective ways of flexing as well. These were early-stage tech companies, representing both B2B and B2C business models. Many of them just accepted hierarchy, while others were resigned to being flat and chaotic. But some of the best-managed companies were able to flex the hierarchy fluidly. Day to day and meeting to meeting, I saw managers who could make the team hierarchical but also flatten it when they needed to. I think realizing how to manage that duality—and allow for autonomy—is at the heart of this. At the end of the day there needs to be a leader, but it doesn't mean every interaction is hierarchical.

Are there special skills managers need to learn?

Companies are realizing that to do hierarchy well, they really need to invest in leadership development. Even startups realize that leadership is a set of behavioral tools that can be learned.

A lot of the companies are also experimenting with different types of structures, where project teams are flatter but report regularly to a panel of internal company advisers (as opposed to leaders). The trouble is that a lot of these experiments are not data driven. They don't collect large-scale data to see whether the infrastructure actually works.

One experiment that has received a fair amount of exposure is known as holacracy. It was introduced by management at Zappos, the online shoe retailer, in 2013, where it was used to scale back hierarchy in favor of flat, cross-functional groups. In the course of the experiment, Zappos discovered that it needed an elaborate rule book to guide people on how to use the holacratic method. In fact, it was much more complicated than the hierarchy they'd started off with. When the CEO, Tony Hsieh, gave employees the option of accepting the new system or leaving the company, one-third of them walked out.[3] Since then, Zappos has made a bunch of changes but has maintained some aspects of the system. Although I think ideas like holacracy have value, in my view imposing rigid schemes is the wrong way to go.

As for other approaches, there are aspects of agile that have shown promise. But companies still need to figure out how to allow for moments of hierarchy. Members of agile teams still need to coordinate and find ways to resolve conflicts. Even if you're not using hierarchy, you always need a decision-making role. The question is, how can you encourage working together and coordination in a simple and elegant manner?

So where does this leave managers? Do they keep looking for good alternatives to hierarchy or focus on the flexible flattening you've described?

Until we have an alternative model that is established and has been shown to work, the simplest and safest approach for companies is to use hierarchy but also to train leaders to use it well: to be able to flex and adapt how they use it. This means selecting leaders who have the skill sets to foster teams that are empowered and hierarchical, while training both leaders and teams how to adapt the hierarchical structure to handle the demands.

11

Why Teams Should Record Individual Expectations

Ken Favaro and Manish Jhunjhunwala

With all the performance troubles at GE over the past couple of years, one problem stands out: Corporate executives were regularly making promises to shareholders about revenue and profits that operating managers knew were impossible. According to the *Wall Street Journal*, GE had developed "a culture that disdained bad news [and] contributed to overoptimistic forecasts and botched strategies." Billions of dollars of value destruction might have been avoided had management's decisions been better informed by the insights and expectations of its employees closer to the ground.

That may sound like a tall order, especially for such a large organization, given the logistics of wrangling staffers at multiple levels, recording the numbers they expect from upcoming projects, consolidating their input, and then meeting (sometimes repeatedly) to align forecasts and inform planning. But when we had to evaluate a potential partnership at Trefis (where one of us, Manish, is the CEO, and the other, Ken, consults), the team hit upon a surprisingly manageable method for recording and analyzing individuals' expectations that has improved decision making and risk management, and has even informed the central offering to clients. Granted, most companies—Trefis included—are not the size of GE, but the process we're talking about is fairly straightforward for teams to implement, and it can be scaled from there.

Here's how we stumbled on it: We knew the partnership we were considering had great potential to expand our customer base. But as we updated our investors and directors, we began to realize that our expectations were widely divergent. We had several different versions of how much growth was possible and of how to get there—and, of course, our views changed as we exchanged contrasting scenarios. This made it hard to tackle decisions such as how to price our service to the partner's customers and how many support people to deploy on the account.

After about six months, to improve alignment, we developed a basic spreadsheet to capture everyone's individual volume, price, and revenue expectations for the partnership. We entered the historical data from the first two quarters of pilot projects and allocated space to record projections for the business we might do over the next five quarters. We converted that spreadsheet into an interactive dashboard and sent a hyperlink to our investors, directors, and top executives—and to employees involved in the partnership—so they could each enter their projections. Everyone could see the collective results and where the variances were, in graph form. It helped us quickly identify areas that needed further discussion before sound decisions could be made.

Now, any time we meet to discuss the partnership, we consult our dashboard. We can tinker with individual expectations and see how those adjustments would change the mean and the variance. That makes it easier to understand where the group stands. Perhaps more important, every stakeholder feels heard and better aware of others' viewpoints.

For three reasons, we have since adopted this practice for a whole range of decisions, including pricing, sales and marketing resource deployment, new-product priorities, and broader strategic choices.

1. Decision alignment and quality improve when you record expectations. We shared our experience with more than 30 Fortune 500 and private equity executives to gain their views on the idea of systematically collecting expectations for important decisions. In those interviews, we heard one story over and over: Standard practice is to seek a consensus view with an upside and downside case. But it's extremely rare that members of a decision-making group know and discuss their respective expectations. As a result, executives told us, it's common to have the appearance of alignment on a decision, when just below the surface a slew of different and potentially informative views are bubbling away.

However, when individual expectations are recorded along with the key assumptions behind them, important differences become visible. One person might see $2 + 2$ as the problem to solve, another might see $1 + 3$, and another might think it's $5 - 1$. Even if you all arrive at the same answer, recording and then discussing the variety of paths that different stakeholders expect forces everyone to think in new ways. And often the team ends up concluding that $1 + 5$ is the right starting place—and thus arriving at a different, unanticipated, and better decision altogether.

This was borne out by our experience with the decision we faced on a go-to-market partnership. Our product and sales teams disagreed on whether we should partner or go it alone. Creating expectations dashboards for each option put our discussions on firmer footing, and we came up with a third option that appealed to everyone: Go all in with the partner, but negotiate for higher net pricing from the partner as certain milestones are reached.

2. Looking only at past outcomes is a flawed way to manage risk. Companies tend to measure the risks of pending decisions by looking at outcomes of past decisions because those results are known. Analysts pore over everything, including profit, margins, volume, price, and cost, and use those data points to assess the new decision's prospects. This approach has two flaws. First, risk is context-dependent, and the current situation may present entirely different obstacles or constraints. Second, for a backward-looking assessment to be truly valuable, you need a big sample of outcomes from relevant decisions made in the past. It's rare for a company to have a statistically significant number of those to draw on—and the bigger the decision in front of you, the more likely this is the case.

Gathering independent expectations from each stakeholder shifts everyone's focus to the real point of interest: how the decision at hand is likely to play out in the future. Those expectations are still essentially guesses, but they're tied to the appropriate context; they're coming from informed parties; and they reflect a variety of perspectives, which helps to hedge against individual biases and groupthink.

By considering a range of expectations on key inputs, leaders and their teams can also better anticipate where surprises—both positive and negative—might alter a desired outcome. One private equity executive told us that before making deals, he wants to see what his team members expect for deal parameters such as exit multiples and follow-on acquisitions, as well as for metrics on sales expenditures and EBITDA growth. Only when he has that data can he really get a sense of whether and when to participate in a venture. In our decision making, we collect expectations for different metrics but with a similar goal: getting the fullest possible picture of the risks we face.

3. Leaders and their teams grow as decision-makers when they record expectations. While a dashboard can simplify the process of recording and analyzing expectations, it cannot erase the human element. It cannot force people who fear constructive disagreement to volunteer their estimates. It cannot comfort someone whose expectations often vary widely from the rest of the team's. Only leaders can address those issues—and to do so, they must recognize that decision making is a skill. People need feedback to develop it. Having information on how the expectations behind your decisions panned out gives you that feedback.

Recording expectations and comparing them against actual results over time can reveal a leader's or team's habitual biases and blind spots. For example, executives at a global life sciences company based in Switzerland commissioned a comprehensive study comparing outcomes of decisions with the expectations that went into them. According to its corporate strategy executive, that assessment of decision quality across initiatives helped even the most intuitive leaders improve their "decision batting average." The company is now planning to conduct a similar study every year.

Making better decisions takes practice. You may have to push to make recording expectations an accepted routine in your organization. Even though it's not as taxing as we initially assumed, it still takes time, and there's cultural work to do. To facilitate buy-in, we've found it's important to clearly articulate the benefits and make it safe for individuals to lay their expectations bare. Positive leadership can help show employees how recording and analyzing data leads to more inclusive—and therefore better—decision making.

12

Collaborate Smarter, Not Harder

Rob Cross, Thomas H. Davenport, and Peter Gray[1]

No question, in a competitive global landscape, collaboration allows companies to serve exacting clients more seamlessly, respond more quickly to changing environments, and innovate more rapidly. But when an organization tries to boost collaboration by adopting a new formal structure, technology, or way of working, it often adds a steady stream of time- and energy-consuming interactions to an already relentless workload, diminishing instead of improving performance.

Think about the consequences at an individual level: It's not unusual to feel as if we are just starting our work at 5 p.m., after the daily battery of demands has finally quieted down. Thanks to the plethora of technologies that keep us connected, increasingly integrated global operations, and the need for a multidisciplinary approach to deploying complex products and services, the problem has snowballed over the past decade, with collaborative time demands rising more than 50%. Most knowledge workers and leaders spend 85% or more of their time on email, in meetings, and on the phone.[2] Employees struggle with increases in email volume, the proliferation of new collaborative tools, and expectations of fast replies to messages—with deleterious effects on their quality of work and efficiency. Research tells us that simple distractions like checking a text message fragment our attention more than we realize, and more consuming distractions—such as answering an email—can cost us more than 20 minutes to fully regain our focus.[3]

Even though employees are acutely aware that they're suffering, most organizations don't recognize what's happening in the aggregate. "We can track an airline receipt down to two decimal places and create a whole infrastructure around compliance, but we have no idea how effective networks are or where collaborative time is being spent," lamented the CIO of one company we studied. With increasing pressure on organizations to become more agile, there is also a greater tendency to swamp employees with collaboration demands in pursuit of a networked organization. We have found that people have, on average, at least nine different technologies to manage their interactions with work groups. The result can be overwhelmed and unproductive employees, sapped creativity, and employee attrition.

Fortunately, it is possible to improve collaboration efforts with the help of analytics. Perhaps the first industry to do so was professional basketball, where quantitative analysts realized that some players scored relatively little but somehow made their teammates more successful.[4] Similar analysis has been deployed by professional soccer teams to identify what patterns of passing were most effective for scoring goals under particular circumstances.[5] But the benefits of understanding patterns of collaboration can be reaped in all kinds of organizations.

Using analytics to make collaborative activities more transparent helps companies identify and exploit previously invisible drivers of revenue production, innovation, and employee effectiveness. Analytics enables better management of what has become an enormous yet hidden cost for organizations, one that employees aren't equipped to manage on their own.

Five Ways Businesses Can Benefit

In our research on collaboration over the past decade, we have seen some effective uses of analytics emerge in two industry consortia, where we've identified whether collaborations are driving value or unintentionally consuming resources.[6] These organizations have gone beyond documenting simple collaborative activities—who talks to whom at what frequency—to systematically relating collaborative activities to key outcomes.

In particular, we found five main ways in which companies derive value from collaboration analytics. First, they scale collaboration effectively by deploying targeted analytics to connect critical roles (for instance, project leads and first-line leaders) and to link employees engaged in similar work who are distributed across functions, units, or geographies. Second, organizations improve collaborative design and execution by understanding how networks cross hierarchies and team structures, and by replicating drivers of success. Third, they use collaborative analytics to drive planned and emergent innovation through networks that cross capabilities, markets, or functions. Fourth, the insights they glean from analytics allow them to streamline collaborative work by diagnosing and reducing collaborative overload and removing unnecessary routine decision-making interactions. Fifth, companies engage talent by using collaboration analytics to identify social capital enablers of performance, engagement, and retention.

We'll explore each source of value in turn.

1. Scaling collaboration effectively. Most organizations have developed deep talent in knowledge-intensive core capabilities, but it's much less common that those individuals with expertise are systematically connected to one another. They can be far-flung throughout the organization, often distributed across functions, geographies, and P&Ls, which means that no single leader or unit is responsible for deriving benefits from their collaborations. As a result, scale benefits are often very limited.

Collaboration analytics, however, can maximize the benefits of scale in three key areas:

- **Around specific leadership roles**—typically first-level and manager of manager—for which failure rates have a significant impact on the organization.
- **Across strategically important functional roles**—or pivot roles[7]—that have a disproportionate impact on execution or innovation processes.
- **Within communities of core technical experts**—whether scientific-, engineering-, or software-related—that a company relies on for strategic capability.

Take, for example, General Electric, which has an enormous knowledge base in its more than 300,000 employees around the globe, across nine businesses. Prior to 2015, GE's efforts to link distributed pockets of expertise were uneven. "We had bright spots where cross-business expertise sharing was working, but we were not consistent within and across segments. It was limiting our scale opportunities," noted knowledge-sharing leader Dan Ranta. Leaders saw the opportunity to improve collaboration across the company through new analytics-powered expertise communities. The goal was to enable expertise integration in a natural way that would require little effort from the experts involved.

Ranta and his team first developed a quantitative model to predict whether a given community was ready to share its expertise globally, on the basis of data collected about successful knowledge-sharing communities elsewhere in the company. They calculated scores that reflected the maturity of collaboration among community members, their degree of mutual commitment to success, the extent to which their local technological environment would support a global community, and the level of support for a global community within their organization. When the model predicted that a community was ready, Ranta's team included that community in a new knowledge-sharing architecture featuring discussion spaces where experts could interact globally. Those that were not ready were steered instead toward smaller and more focused structures, such as mission-based teams.

GE used analytics to predict which community member would have the right expertise to answer each kind of question and, through industrial-scale software, to automatically distribute questions to the appropriate community experts. For community management purposes, GE generated real-time analytics of collaboration patterns to identify the employees who were most engaged and making a difference across locations.

As a result of this work, GE's expertise is becoming easier to tap, wherever it resides. For example, GE's Renewable Energy business, with approximately 43,000 employees, has deployed 27 communities to connect individuals across hundreds of technical discussions that span geographical and business boundaries, collectively producing a vast array of solutions and learnings. In one year, 1,172 internal collaborators collectively solved a total of 513 customer problems, resulting in more than $1.1 million of cost avoidance in productivity. "Analytics powers our processes, minimizes the human cost of helping each other out, and lets us tap into the thickest vein in the 'gold mine of sharing,' which is human generosity and professional pride," Ranta noted.

2. Improving collaborative design and execution. Team-based structures are common in organizations, but employees assigned to too many teams end up slowing efforts and creating significant disruption if they burn out and leave.[8] Collaboration analytics can help leaders determine where team structures are most effective, informing in-house training and generating best practices that help replicate those networks and tune teams for agility and speed.

Lateral collaboration is particularly challenging in investment banking firms. Despite often advocating a "one firm" culture, the hierarchies that grow under a partner often lead employees to concentrate all of their efforts within their teams, while time constraints further limit their ability to learn about solutions available from other partner silos. This can lead client-facing teams to focus on selling their own solutions rather than integrated, holistic solutions that command higher margins and improve client retention.

Executives at one global investment bank realized that this partner-silo structural dilemma was preventing their firm from catching up to industry leaders. Through a network analysis, an analytics team quantified the number of revenue-producing ties among midtier team leaders to understand where integrated offerings based on bundles of skills were—and were not—happening.

The team discovered an asset that had been overlooked: midtier employees who enabled others to cross-sell services. Compared with other employees, these "hidden integrators" had three times as many ties across partner groups, and their connections were almost five times more likely to link poorly connected teams. Financially, these hidden integrators accounted for more than six times the average cross-selling revenue.

But it turned out that in spite of their tremendous value to the firm, these hidden integrators were actually at risk. Several had recently departed the firm. Analytics revealed that they were underappreciated: Their impact on cross-selling was largely invisible to the company and not counted toward revenue generation. Leaders quickly adjusted the compensation system to acknowledge their critical contributions.

Perhaps most important, analytics revealed that these valuable integrators were successful in different ways. Some integrators specialized in enabling many smaller transactions, so the firm freed up their time for this. Other integrators excelled at enabling much larger transactions (more than $15 million), but because these occurred much less frequently, these employees had to be managed and rewarded differently for their longer-term efforts.

3. Driving planned and emergent innovation. Innovation is inherently a social process, grounded in the creative friction that comes when people with different types of expertise and experiences pull one another in unexpected directions and arrive at something entirely new. Understanding where an organization should stimulate innovation by building networks that bring together people with different kinds of expertise is not something best left to chance. Collaboration analytics can uncover silos across capabilities that—if better integrated—could spur innovation and translate creative ideas into production-ready offerings.

General Motors used collaboration analytics to do just that. Radically new business models are emerging in the automobile industry for shared mobility, autonomous driving, electrification, and connectivity. In the face of such opportunities and an unprecedented set of nontraditional competitors, GM recognized that it had to take bold actions to adapt to this new world.

GM rapidly acquired startups and hired new talent to boost its technological capabilities in core strategic areas. But despite these investments in GM's *human* capital, executives also recognized the importance of *social* capital, or the networks of ties that connect employees and amplify their individual capabilities. To produce a dramatic increase in the company's agility and innovativeness, GM focused on creating what then-chief talent officer Michael Arena termed *adaptive space*—a network of connections that link the entrepreneurial pockets of innovation within the company to its traditional execution-focused operational elements.[9] This began to chip away at historic silos. Creating adaptive space required interventions around four different kinds of networks: idea discovery, concept development, innovation diffusion, and organizational disruption. Although all were important, let's focus on the second stage—concept development—in which promising ideas were rapidly developed into emergent innovations.

Arena asked the internal analytics team to study the networks of two development groups that transformed ideas into novel prototypes. One was better at this than the other. Collaboration analytics derived from network data revealed that the more successful group had a clustering coefficient (the degree to which a group consists of small, tightly knit subgroups) that was more than two times higher than that of its less successful counterpart. The more successful group was better at forming small subgroups that collaborated on a single task or function of the overall development challenge. That way, they were able to concentrate on perfecting one thing at a time and make rapid, focused progress.

As you might expect, the successful group also had a density metric (a measure based on how many ties link a group together) almost double that of the less successful group. Through these ties, team members tasked with one aspect of development shared their advancements with members from other clusters in ways that helped combine local innovations into a functioning, broader automotive concept. Interestingly, while the successful network had more internal ties, its members had fewer external ties to potential idea sources in industry or academia, so they were free from outside distractions that could hinder their focus on the task at hand throughout development. The less successful development group had more external connections, which were valuable in enabling discovery of new insights but often led the team to hedge their development bets by simultaneously pursuing multiple different possibilities. Ironically, this had a negative impact on the speed of concept development and prolonged the decision to shut down less successful prototypes.

The combination of acquiring skilled employees and ensuring that these individuals are properly positioned in the network has enabled GM to adapt faster to the disruptive forces that surround it.

4. Streamlining collaborative work. As employees spend more of their time in meetings, on phone calls, and on email, collaboration analytics can play a powerful role in identifying where excessive connectivity is draining time, slowing speed to market, or hurting employee morale. Collaboration overload can beset specific individuals or roles, and collaboration analytics can identify the situations where some people are collaboratively far less efficient than others in the organization.[10] Sometimes overload is created through excessively inclusive decision processes. In general, overload occurs when more than a quarter of the people who interact with any individual employee report (through an internal survey) that they cannot improve their own performance without more access to that individual.

Perhaps nowhere is streamlining collaborative work more important than in the commercialization of new pharmaceuticals. Commercialization occurs after most of the enormous investments required to develop a new drug have been made but before the product hits the shelves. It is extraordinarily time-sensitive, with a single day's delay costing the company millions in lost profits. But drug commercialization is also incredibly collaboration-intensive, requiring orchestration among regulatory affairs, medical affairs, R&D, sales, marketing, legal, advocacy, manufacturing, and many other functions.

Streamlining collaboration can have a direct and immediate effect on the bottom line. The leader of a drug commercialization unit in one pharmaceutical company we studied discovered that truth after using collaboration analytics to identify opportunities to increase efficiency of routine decision making, which often seemed to be taking too long. The analytics team asked each member of the commercialization group to answer a series of questions about his or her network of collaborators, including how much time each spent in routine versus nonroutine decisions. Armed with data about the estimated delay these types of decisions caused, the team used text analytics to calculate which categories of decisions delayed the process the longest.

Focusing on each area of opportunity for improvement, leaders and their staffs drafted guidelines for optimal decision making, in some cases developing decision-flow schematics to ensure that all parties involved knew the best sequence and time lines. They revised governance principles and trained employees to push responsibility and accountability down in the organization.

The analytics team also discovered significant variation in how much time individuals spent collaborating with certain roles within the unit and preparing for those interactions (what we term *collaborative efficiency*). Statistical analyses identified four specific roles in which individuals were acting in ways that they may have believed to be efficient but that did not adhere to any standardized best practice. Those who were most efficient in those roles consumed only a small amount of time from each person in his or her network, while those who were least efficient consumed many times as much. Subsequent calculations revealed that improving the latter group's efficiency could have a catalytic effect on the entire organization. Simply bringing it up to average could free up more than 17,000 hours of collaboration time annually in the rest of the organization—*the equivalent of almost nine full-time employees.*

With these insights, the unit was able to recoup thousands of hours and shave time off the overall commercialization process. Analyzing collaboration in this way showed that changes were possible and desirable and provided the diagnostic insights to help other groups in the company discover new and better ways of doing their jobs.

Using survey-based data about collaboration is not the only way to glean useful insights about a company's collaboration inefficiencies. It's also possible to extract collaboration data from existing digital sources, such as meeting and email data, as a by-product of other behaviors. A leading mortgage finance company employed a "passive data" collaboration analytics engine that enabled its analytics team to easily identify opportunities for streamlining. One unit seemed particularly effective, and analysis of passive collaboration data revealed how those employees' behaviors were different from others in the company. This group had created a culture of empowerment and strong working relationships among employees. For instance, they spent 56% less time in approval-related meetings and 29% more time on approval-related emails. They also worked with greater autonomy, spending 20% less time in meetings where their supervisor was present. And they were more focused when in face-to-face collaborations, having 40% fewer meeting conflicts and sending 18% fewer emails while in meetings.

5. Engaging talent. A rapidly developing set of collaboration analytics applications has emerged as a natural extension of the people analytics functions in organizations. Organizations are making quick progress on a variety of thorny talent-related issues—and generating impact in areas where progress has often traditionally been limited—by incorporating social capital drivers of success alongside traditional human capital drivers. For instance, companies are doing the following:

- Reducing attrition through analytics models that identify the collaboration patterns that predict retention.[11]
- Promoting individual performance and transition success by studying networks of high performers and helping others to replicate those networks.[12]

- Refining performance management processes to locate and retain top collaborators whom traditional systems often miss.
- Using evidence-based approaches to generate more impact from diversity and inclusion programs.

Booz Allen Hamilton provides a rare example of the use of predictive collaboration analytics to not just anticipate but also improve employee retention. The company had already developed a predictive attrition model based on data such as demographic attributes, work characteristics, level in the organization, length of service, and compensation and benefits. The model pinpointed key attrition drivers and identified employees at greatest risk of leaving the company who might benefit from targeted interventions. However, after the model was developed, additional social factors that might affect attrition came to light.

Data suggested that the risk for turnover was highest following an employee's transition to a new role. Further analysis revealed that how an employee managed networks shaped the odds of leaving after a transition. Mapping data about the size, reach, and quality of each employee's collaboration network against attrition data uncovered different insights at specific tenure bands. The analysis contradicted much of the traditional advice about networks (for instance, that a big network is always a good network).

Five categories of network-based factors distinguished employees who departed within two years of joining the company from those who stayed. The people who stayed were those who created more energy in their interactions with others, helped others find a sense that their work had purpose and mattered, generated "pull" (or demand) for their talents, created diversity of thought through broader networks, and connected with a strong peer cohort. On the basis of these findings, Booz Allen implemented a new onboarding program that focused on the specific network dimensions that were most likely to increase retention. Follow-up analyses confirmed a significant improvement in retention as a result of the new collaboration training.

A second example involves using collaboration analytics to more efficiently and effectively assess performance management—a key driver of employee engagement[13]—at W. L. Gore & Associates, an R&D-based product development company. The company's flat, latticelike organizational structure empowers associates to decide which leaders to follow and also makes them directly accountable to members of their teams. Without traditional bosses to evaluate performance, team members rate one another on their contributions (impact and effectiveness), which is combined into a ranking of all associates within their areas across the company. The ranking system is then used to determine associates' compensation.

By 2015, Gore had grown to more than 9,000 associates, which greatly increased the complexity of the contribution-evaluation process. The company's global growth meant that many associates were working on multiple colocated and virtual teams, with any single team aware of only a small slice of an associate's performance. As a result, evaluating contributions could take many days to complete for a single associate, particularly for those individuals who were central to the networks of performance in the company.

Gore began to explore a more streamlined, two-pronged approach, using collaboration analytics. First, automated surveys empowered individual associates to nominate network contacts who knew their contributions best. An algorithm ingested all this collaboration data and revealed which associates were in

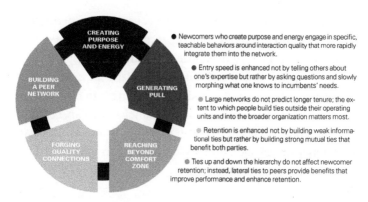

Network Drivers of Retention at Booz Allen Hamilton
Collaboration data analysis shows that new hires who stay with the company are those who engage in these behaviors.

a position to compare pairs of other associates. A second automated survey then presented each associate with pairings of collaborators they were uniquely suited to evaluate and asked them to rate whether one was a stronger contributor than the other. All this typically took each associate 15 to 20 minutes to complete rather than hours or days. Analytics run on the aggregated dataset then produced rankings for all associates in the company.

For a pilot in a 200-person unit, Gore found that the rankings were highly comparable to those recently generated through the traditional contribution assessment process. The process was fully rolled out in 2017. "Conservatively, we estimated 10,000 hours a year that our approach saved, but in reality, it was probably several multiples of that," noted team member Willis Jensen. Equally important, the new process was still well aligned with the company's empowerment culture.

Despite widespread agreement that collaboration is critical to achieving desired business outcomes, organizations have been flying blind on how to maximize that value under specific circumstances. Too often, well-intended collaboration initiatives have actually been counterproductive, sliding into overload for key employees. With collaboration analytics, we can begin to shed light on who needs to collaborate with whom about what, what types of collaboration yield particular results, and how collaboration affects employee satisfaction, performance, and attrition.

Far beyond traditional analytics that simply provide descriptive, visual models of who talks to whom, a new generation of collaboration analytics is emerging, with more predictive and prescriptive capabilities. These analytics use advanced methods, including machine learning, to identify key data without requiring extra effort from employees and to relate collaboration metrics to a variety of business performance measures. They have the potential to ensure that initiatives designed to help make your team more productive don't backfire spectacularly.

These new approaches are putting collaboration analytics on an even plane with other important analytical tools in organizations. They are bringing the decision-making power of data and analytics to human cooperation at work.

The Research

- The authors spoke with more than 100 managers and executives actively engaged in collaboration analytics projects.
- Their sample was drawn from two industry-based consortia.
- They focused on identifying where collaboration analytics had been used to make evidence-based decisions that affected business performance.

13

Improving the Rhythm of Your Collaboration

Ethan Bernstein, Jesse Shore, and David Lazer

Count-offs at the beginning of musical performances, whether verbal ("One, two . . .") or symbolic (with a baton or a snap), are a fixture of live collaboration for musicians. Conductors use them to establish tempo and feel, and to provide guidance on how to interpret the written rhythms—the patterns of sound and silence—that the ensemble is about to play.

Similarly, in the workplace, leaders help set the beat for their organizations' and teams' collaborative efforts. For at least a century, they have done this largely by planning working-group meetings, huddles, one-on-ones, milestone reports, steering committee readouts, end-of-shift handoffs, and so on. Through 30-, 60-, and 90-minute calendar meetings scheduled weeks in advance to prevent conflicts and at odd times to accommodate global team members, they have established the patterns of active interaction ("sound") and individual work ("silence") that form the rhythms of their employees' collaboration.

But such rhythms have gotten much more complex and less controlled in recent years. Organizations now have a treasure chest of digital tools for collaboration—Slack, Teams/Skype, Chatter, Yammer, Jive, Zoom, Webex, Klaxoon—that they didn't have before. (The global collaboration software market was $8 billion in 2018 and is projected to double to $16 billion by 2025.[1]) Add to that email, texting, and messaging, along with the meetings that haven't gone away, and the math is telling: Research shows that executives spend an average of nearly 23 hours per week in meetings (up from less than 10 hours 50 years ago),[2] while McKinsey & Company estimates the average knowledge worker spends 65% of the workday collaborating and communicating with others (including 28% of the day on email).[3] So collaboration has gone omnichannel. You can see why orchestrating all of this has become such a challenge.

Indeed, given how hyperconnected most people are now at work, one might question whether they even have a rhythm of collaboration, not because they lack sufficient interaction (sound) but because they lack any absence of it (silence). That observation prompted us, as researchers, to ask: *Should* organizations have a rhythm of collaboration that alternates on and off, or is more simply better, as people tend to assume?

Our findings suggest that alternation is essential for work that involves problem solving. As collaborative tools make interaction cheaper and more abundant, opportunities to think *without* interaction are becoming more expensive and scarce, yet they remain critical. In fact, our research shows that when people trade a rhythm of on-and-off collaboration for always-on connectivity, they coordinate and gather information more effectively, but they produce less innovative, less productive solutions.

That's troubling, given current trends in the workplace. By achieving more and more connectivity, humans are becoming a bit like passive nodes in a machine network: They are getting better at processing information but worse at making decisions from it. In other words, we've designed organizational communication to make it harder, not easier, for human beings to do what we're being told we need to do in the next decade or two—that is, differentiate our capabilities from the growing capacities of big data, automation, and AI.

It takes more leadership—not less, as the trend toward flatter organizations and teams might lead us to believe—to create an effective rhythm that alternates between rich interaction and quiet focus. Here, we explore what that means in practice for managers and draw on examples from organizations we've studied to illustrate how you can avoid common problems and establish an optimal collaborative rhythm for your team.

Connectivity: What We Gain, What We Lose

When we solve problems collaboratively—whether we're making strategic decisions, fixing operational glitches, or generating ideas—we engage in two categories of actions: (1) gathering the facts we need to generate and develop various potential solutions, and (2) figuring out the best solutions.

Academics are not strangers to the study of problem solving. There is a large body of research about it, with contexts including recreational venues like adventure racing[4] and escape rooms,[5] simulated laboratory experiments, and real-world field research in the workplace. But most of the research has focused on individual rather than collective problem solving.[6] Even among studies of collaboration, few have looked into how much we want to have.[7]

So we headed to the laboratory to explore that question. In our first study,[8] we randomly assigned individuals to 51 16-person organizations—some more connected by technology than others—and asked each organization to solve a complex

problem: Divine the who, what, where, and when of an impend-
ing terrorist attack (akin to the famous Clue whodunit game
but with higher hypothetical stakes). Each organization used a
platform not unlike the collaborative tools used in workplaces
today: Through their computers, individuals could search for
information, share it with one another, and contribute theories
about solutions while the platform tracked all behavior.

We found that connectivity had different effects on the
fact-finding and figuring stages of problem solving. For finding facts, more connectivity was better, without limitation. But
figuring out what to do with those facts—actually creating the
solutions—was undermined by too much connectedness. The
same connections that helped individuals collaborate in their
search for information also encouraged them to reach consensus on less-than-perfect solutions, making connectivity a true
double-edged sword.

Fact-finding and figuring are, we believe, representative of
broader classes of activities. If we were to describe this trade-off
more generically, it is the question of whether the task primarily
requires coordination or imagination. If there are acute coordination needs (for instance, avoiding redundant effort by ensuring we don't all look under the same pillow for the keys), then
always-on connectivity is helpful. If imagination is more critical,
then always-on connectivity can make it nearly impossible to
manage the creativity of multiple minds, which requires a balance between allowing those minds to learn from one another
and enhancing the capacity of each one to generate fresh ideas.
Too little communication, and there's no learning and no synergy. Too much communication, and all the minds end up in the
same place, focusing on the same types of solutions.

Too little communication, and there's no learning and no synergy. Too much communication, and all the minds end up in the same place, focusing on the same types of solutions.

Breaking the Trade-Off

Does that have to be the case? Do organizations and teams need to choose between being great at fact-finding and being great at figuring?

To further investigate, we returned to the laboratory, this time with the goal of directly asking whether deliberately choosing a rhythm of collaboration (that isn't always on) could help.[9] We asked a number of three-person groups to solve what's called the *traveling salesperson problem*. Each person was given a map with the locations of 25 fictional cities that they needed to visit. Their task was to find the shortest trip to visit each city once and then return home to their starting point.

For decades, academics have been using the traveling salesperson problem to study complex problem solving, in part because the set of all possible solutions forms what is called a *rugged solution landscape*: If you were to visualize all options as paths up a mountain (where the altitude reached is the measure of success), getting from a good solution to a better one might require you to hike back down the mountain and climb a very different path. So myopic decision makers (as we all inevitably are) risk getting stuck at a low peak because they didn't see the higher peak before they started climbing. This happens in the traveling salesperson problem because the choice of which city to visit next is constrained by the other choices made in one's route. To find a better solution, one must often go back and reconfigure those decisions.

In our version of the traveling salesperson problem, people attempted to solve it under one of three conditions. The members of one set of groups never interacted with one another, solving the problem in complete isolation; members of another set constantly interacted, as we do when equipped with always-on technologies; and members of the third set interacted intermittently.

Consistent with our previous study and other research,[10] we anticipated—and found—that the groups with no interaction were the most creative, coming up with the largest number of unique solutions, including some of the best and some of the worst in terms of total distance traveled to visit each city and return back home again. In short, when isolated, they produced a few fantastic solutions but, overall, a low average quality of solution due to so much variation.

We also anticipated—and found—that the groups with constant interaction were the most consistent, producing a higher average quality of solution but finding the very best ones much less frequently. In other words, when always on, they produced less variable but more mediocre solutions.

Groups that interacted intermittently—with a true rhythm of collaboration—broke the tradeoff, capturing the best of both worlds rather than succumbing to the worst of either one. They preserved enough isolation to find the best solutions at least as frequently as the groups with no interaction, but also enough collaboration to maintain an equivalently high average quality of solution compared with the groups with constant interaction.

Learning was a key factor: During periods of separation, people naturally struck out on their own and tried new and diverse approaches to the problem—but when they came together again, they could learn from these different solutions. Even if the new solutions people found on their own weren't effective overall, they often included a useful idea or two that could be learned from and recombined with other solutions. In this sense, intermittent interaction created the conditions for collective intelligence, rather than relying on a few leading individuals to come up with the strongest ideas.

Even people with the best solution at any given point in the experiment did better in an intermittent environment. They were exposed to new ideas from their peers that they could use to improve their already good solutions. And of course, people with worse solutions could adopt the best solution in the group as a new jumping-off point for their next period of solo solving.

By contrast, people who interacted constantly had many opportunities to learn but fewer ideas to learn from, given how closely they hewed to group consensus. Those who never interacted generated more (and more diverse) ideas, but their isolation prevented learning from occurring.

There are two key lessons for managers in those results. First, when it comes to solving complex problems, collaboration yields diminishing returns—beyond a certain point, the average quality of solutions does not improve from more interaction. Second, too much collaboration has its costs—you drive out the diversity of thought that is helpful for creating the best solutions.[11]

Finding the Right Rhythm at Work

Clearly there's value in having a rhythm of collaboration rather than always-on interaction. But how do you choose one and then put it into practice? What's the equivalent of a musician's count-off by the leader of an organization or team? Here are a few approaches that seem promising in light of our research.

The light switch approach: Turn it off – in cycles. As with so many things, collaboration technology has simultaneously solved one

The fear of being left out of the loop can keep people glued to their enterprise social media. They don't want to be – or appear to be – isolated.

problem (too little interaction) and created another (too much). Our research and that of others[12] suggests that it's important to find opportunities to unplug not just off-hours but also during work. Many of us eagerly anticipate the time we get to spend in the quiet car of the train, on an airplane with no Wi-Fi, or in a cabin that is just a bit too remote to be on the grid. Leaders can provide that kind of time in the workplace, too. While people are getting used to putting smartphones in a box on their way into a meeting (to focus on one form of collaboration versus another), more and more organizations are also creating coordinated unplugged times for heads-down work.

Flicking the collaboration light switch is something that leaders are uniquely positioned to do, because several obstacles stand in the way of people voluntarily working alone. For one thing, the fear of being left out of the loop can keep them glued to their enterprise social media. Individuals don't want to be—or appear to be—isolated. For another, knowing what their teammates are doing provides a sense of comfort and security, because people can adjust their own behavior to be in sync with the group. It's risky to go off on their own to try something new that will probably not be successful right from the start. But even though it feels reassuring for individuals to be hyperconnected, it's better for the organization if they periodically go off and think for themselves and generate diverse—if not quite mature—ideas. Thus, it becomes the leader's job to create conditions that are good for the whole by enforcing intermittent interaction even when people wouldn't choose it for themselves, without making it seem like a punishment (such as a time-out from childhood).

In some companies, unplugging is enabled by physical spaces and norms that prohibit collaboration. Meditation rooms and meditation coaches, for example, are on the rise—not just at

Apple, where Steve Jobs introduced the 30-minute daily meditation break, but also at companies as varied as Google, Nike, Pearson, and Nationwide. At Amazon, instead of jumping right into a collaborative review of bullet points on PowerPoint slides, meetings may start with people sitting silently while reading a memo, discussing the topic only after everyone is done reading.

But it's not enough to provide space and permission for quiet focus. Role modeling by leaders is key. In an age in which it is transparent to others when you are plugged in (messaging systems indicate whether you are online, how recently you were, and whether you've read a received message), leaders send clear signals with their own behavior. At the most recent Wharton People Analytics Conference, former CEO of Deloitte US Cathy Engelbert said she realized how closely people watch leaders for cues when an employee leaving the company (someone she didn't even know) said that she "didn't want to be like Cathy Engelbert," working and available to interact with colleagues "at all hours." The employee had inferred this—correctly or incorrectly—from repeatedly seeing that Engelbert's instant messaging status was online at night. Unless leaders themselves visibly unplug, meditation rooms and their ilk may become the latest equivalent of the dot-com foosball table, getting used by people who are the most likely to be laid off during the next downturn.

Other companies are placing stricter limits on the time colleagues can spend interacting. At the Italian headquarters of one of the world's top fashion houses, the office goes dark at 5:30 p.m., forcing an end to the workday. In part, the CEO tells us, that is out of respect to the families who await his employees' arrival home. But it also signals an end to collaboration and a start to individual time, something cherished at a company that depends so heavily on creativity. While 5:30 p.m. may be an unrealistic cutoff in many settings, leaders can apply the same basic idea in more targeted ways, for a shorter period of time or even staggered across individuals or teams, as was the case with Boston Consulting Group's Predictable Time Off initiative.[13]

The underlying principle here is not new. One of the most seminal academic studies of work time in the 1990s showed how a software engineering team could reduce their feelings of having a "time famine" and improve productivity by instituting a policy of mandated quiet time, when interruptions were prohibited.[14] Today, that simply means having work time when all our collaboration tools are turned off, taking us back to the days when we naturally had an ebb and flow of collaboration—individual work time punctuated by scheduled meetings and calls.

Agile approaches to teamwork incorporate some of this intermittent cycling, given that they are organized into short sprints during which groups of people focus on solving a particular problem. Harvard Business School professor Andy Wu and his coauthor Sourobh Ghosh have termed this *iterative coordination*.[15] The challenge is that, as one executive at a large financial institution told us, "our sprints have gotten so compressed together that there is no downtime in between them." Plus, just because a team is sprinting doesn't mean others in the organization won't interrupt individual members of the team with collaboration needs that have nothing to do with the sprint.

Hackathons also involve intense collaboration for relatively short, predetermined periods of time. Because they are often organization-wide events—or at least everyone in the organization tends to know about them—they are somewhat more immune to interruption by colleagues, especially when they are sponsored by senior leaders (which provides implicit permission for out-of-office auto replies). But hackathons offer space and time for collaborative innovation—not for quiet, individual work. Leaders must find other ways of bringing that into employees' day-to-day rhythm by literally or figuratively flicking off the lights at regular intervals.

Executives have been counseled to be collaborative leaders and to set the example at the top that they want to see in the rest of the organization.[16] They have taken this message seriously, transparently devoting more and more of their days to in-person and online collaboration. By role modeling such ubiquitous use of collaboration technology, business leaders have helped define an era of always-on collaboration. It is now time to role model a more sustainable, productive rhythm of collaboration.

Even some of the tools' creators are advocating this approach: Ryan Singer, one of the first four employees at Basecamp, a maker of project management software, has written a book (collaboratively online) based on 16+ years of watching companies struggle with project-based collaboration. In it, he writes that "there can be an odd kind of radio silence" during the first phase of effective project work, "because each person has their head down" getting oriented, finding the best approach, and engaging in exploration—doing what he calls "legitimate work." He claims that it is "important for managers to respect this phase [because] asking for visible progress will only push it underground."[17]

The Fitbit approach: Track it to hack it. It will not come as news to anyone that workplace collaboration tools do not just enable collaboration, they also track it. The result of all the time we spend collaborating online, and increasingly in person, is a stream of digital exhaust that defines what's recently been termed *relationship analytics*.[18]

This goes beyond weekly reports on how much screen time we've had, instead capturing each individual's precise rhythms of collaboration with others in the organization. For example, Microsoft now offers two tools that use email, calendar, contacts, and other Office 365 data to provide insights about collaboration: MyAnalytics (for individuals) reports on how responsive you are to collaborators' emails (on average and with specific individuals), reminds you to book focus time "before meetings take over," highlights the "impact of your after-hours emails" on others, and so on; and Workplace Analytics (for an organization) uses the same data, anonymized, to shed light on overall collaboration trends. Ambit Analytics, a spin-off of the team at the Stanford Research Institute that developed Siri's voice algorithms, captures your voice profile and then, during times of active collaboration, can track in real time how well you and your collaborators take turns (total number of turns, average turn length, longest turn length) and how each of your voices will be perceived by others (a so-called tonal analysis that shows when each collaborator sounds fearful, angry, joyous, sad, analytical, confident, or tentative).

In the not-so-distant future, we expect that similar tools will draw on large datasets and machine learning algorithms to seek to directly solve the challenges we highlighted above. Your device will remind you to make your collaboration more intermittent when your solutions seem to lack sufficient diversity and encourage you to come back together and learn from one another when enough diversity has been generated. Artificial intelligence may help us improve our collective intelligence by coaching us on how to regulate our collaboration.

Although that lies in the future, the promise of these tracking tools is already evident. Just as our Fitbit encourages more physical activity by making our current activity levels visible, these tools affect our collaboration behaviors by making those visible.

The design approach: Create enlightened collaboration tools. Both solutions above rely on us to change our own behavior, and that's hard. If it were easy to regulate our rhythms of interaction, we wouldn't be sleeping with our smartphones.[19] But the same tools that permit us to become addicted to interaction can, if designed well, also help us make it intermittent rather than constant.

Some of this has already happened naturally. Consider Slack, a tool that was initially designed on the premise that all communications would be visible to the entire organization, encouraging immediate responses and constant connectivity. Under tremendous pressure from its user base, Slack soon changed its stance and created private channels, which now account for a majority of the collaboration in most work spaces. It also created a status function that allows you to signal when you are offline for one of any number of reasons. Indeed, while we are not aware of any social enterprise software programs that initially offered a feature allowing users to indicate whether they are available or not, nearly all of them have such a feature now. These changes allow for more "off" time and give tacit permission for more intermittent involvement.

The next generation of these programs is trying to go a step further by improving the rhythms of collaboration in live meetings rather than replacing them. Matthieu Beucher, founder and CEO of Klaxoon, intentionally developed Klaxoon with this goal in mind, because meetings themselves can be sources of intermittent interaction. Here's how it works: Meeting participants connect to Klaxoon with their own devices (cellphones, iPads, laptops) even if they are colocated. They then select an activity (brainstorm, poll, questions, decisions, and so on) that supports the group's immediate task or objective. Depending on the activity they select, the tool sets a particular rhythm of collaboration. In some cases, information and ideas are visualized for all to see immediately; in others, data is stored so that the group can make decisions after a period of reflection or, at the very least, after everyone in the meeting has contributed their views. Beucher likens each meeting to a new song and says Klaxoon is designed "to provide different tools to improve collaboration for different parts of the song." As Klaxoon has evolved, it has given users more room for intermittent interaction. For example, it now allows people to turn off the user-identification and time-stamp features so that they can collaborate on their own terms and avoid judgment, by peers or bosses, about when or how much they are or are not collaborating.

The promise of the design approach to balancing separation and connectedness—of using technology to create constraints that permit, nudge, or enforce intermittent interaction—is to make creative and productive skunk works types of teams routine rather than rare self-organized phenomena. For this approach to come into its own, however, we need to know more than we do today. In general, the world has asked technology companies to create tools that enable collaboration as much as possible—and that's what they've done.

How to enable intermittent collaboration is a different problem to solve. The best ideas for doing so are most likely yet to come—perhaps after technology companies learn more about how the customers who buy and use their products create their own work-arounds to add intermittency to these tools.

The world has asked technology companies to create tools that enable collaboration as much as possible – and that's what they've done. How to enable intermittent collaboration is a different problem to solve.

Sociologist Georg Simmel once wrote, "Usually, we only perceive as bound that which we have first isolated in some way. If things are to be joined they must first be separated. . . . Directly as well as symbolically, bodily as well as spiritually, we are continually separating our bonds and binding our separations." Intermittent collaboration may be not only productive but also inherently human.

And yet, to achieve it, we must overcome our equally human impulses to stay connected in a world increasingly marked by omnichannel collaboration.[20] Leaders can play a significant role in providing the policies, data, and tools to establish a productive rhythm of communication.

It's also a collective challenge. To return to our music analogy, leaders essentially do the conducting—but every team member affects how the collaborative rhythm is played. So culture becomes a critical reinforcing factor. Unless individuals feel safe to intermittently disconnect and see that behavior modeled and rewarded by the leaders around them, they're more likely to stay too connected, no matter what their managers say they expect and what kinds of tools and opportunities they provide.

The Research

In one experiment, the authors randomly assigned 51 groups of 16 people into four different network structures and asked them to solve a complex whodunit task, all using collaborative technology but with varying levels of connectivity.

In a second experiment, they randomly assigned 514 sets of three subjects to one of three levels of collaborative interaction (none, intermittent, or constant) and asked the group to solve the classic traveling salesperson problem, which is a complex optimization task.

They also reviewed the literature on information sharing in social networks, collective intelligence, brainstorming, and group and team problem solving.

III

Managing Organizations

14

Reframing the Future of Work

Jeff Schwartz, John Hagel III, Maggie Wooll, and Kelly Monahan

When it comes to the future of work, many organizations are missing the point. Executives are creating new future-of-work initiatives every day, but to what end? Many of these initiatives suffer from being too reactive. For instance, managers may feel pressure to reduce costs by 20%, or the board might ask what the company is doing with machine learning and AI—but there are bigger and better goals leaders can aim for, and it's a critical time for organizations to focus their efforts. Imagine the benefits of a future-of-work strategy aimed at generating more value and meaning for the customer, the workforce, and other partners, and greater earnings for the company over time.

Yet far too many initiatives are focused on incremental gains or efficiency-boosting activities. Robotic process automation, AI, and machine learning are treated as shiny new tools, ones that companies can implement for cutting costs and doing work faster and with less human labor. When organizations subscribe to this narrow perspective, the work of tomorrow will be the same as the work of today.

The real opportunity presented in the future of work goes beyond doing more of the same labor faster and cheaper. The big opportunity for companies is to expand notions of value beyond just cost to the company. Companies have additional levers to explore new sources of value and meaning in order to remain competitive amid rapidly changing market dynamics.

To succeed at this vision of creating greater and varied types of value, organizations must shift in two ways. First, moving beyond cost as a driver to value and meaning expands the kind of impact to aim for. Second, by shifting focus from company to customer, workforce, and company, companies can expand the scope of impact. This framework (see "Future-of-Work Drivers") illustrates the drivers that guide decision making and action (for example: How do we redesign work and workplace? How do we leverage alternative workforce arrangements? How do we implement AI?) and help determine how much time, effort, and attention is directed to particular future-of-work strategies.

Future-of-Work Drivers

This framework looks at the question "the future of work, to what end?" from the perspective of customers, workforces, and companies (rows). Three primary drivers (columns) – cost, value, and meaning – shape the decision making used to achieve these ends.

	COST: Seek to Optimize Efficiency	VALUE: Seek to Expand Opportunities	MEANING: Seek to Make a Difference That Matters/ Motivates
Customers	Acquire product or service for minimal resources	Satisfy known and unmet needs	Achieve aspirations for oneself and others
Workforce	Reduce time and effort required for work	Develop skills/ capabilities for future advancement	Connect to a larger purpose and do work that achieves more of my potential
Company	Operate faster and cheaper	Grow revenues and expand margins	Articulate a purpose that matters across stakeholders

Future-of-Work Drivers: Balancing Cost, Value, and Meaning

Today, most organizations are focused primarily on costs for the company, which puts them in the bottom-left section of the Future-of-Work Drivers framework. We propose that there is untapped potential in moving both vertically and horizontally, to consider not just costs but value and meaning, and shift from a company-centered perspective to one that considers customers, the wider workforce, and other stakeholders as well.

This isn't to say that companies must balance all of these drivers and perspectives all the time—to do so would be unrealistic. But organizations should recognize the broader range of actions that may affect the customer and the workforce in ways that ultimately drive financial results for the company. Customers drive economic markets, while workers drive talent markets, and companies must adapt to each. Future-of-work strategies and the benefits derived will be a function of costs, value, and meaning creation. Organizations focused on implementing technologies to create newfound growth, value, and meaning will be the front-runners in the future of work.

Let's examine this new approach from the three future-of-work drivers.

Cost. From the company perspective, cost means: How do we use the future of work as a way to operate faster and cheaper to the benefit of the organization's bottom line? The focus on faster and cheaper might support a strategy where the customer is also exclusively focused on cost. By assuming the customer cares only about cost, this becomes a game of diminishing returns, where today's gains are quickly competed away. Within these types of companies, the cost-focus and scarcity mindset extend into the workforce, where individual workers seek to reduce their own effort and time against a given amount of work, not necessarily to the benefit of the company. Decisions are top-down, and workforce interactions are transactional and unlikely to lead to new opportunities or innovations.

Focusing only on cost for the company, customer, and worker is a zero-sum game. As discovered in previous organizational performance research, you don't drive profits by cutting cost. Instead, companies should find ways to earn higher prices or higher volume, which requires additional levers to be pulled. As decades of research suggest, solely competing on costs will leave organizations wanting in the future of work.

Value. Value is an additive driver that seeks to expand opportunities. For companies, value often means revenue growth through entering new markets or expanding margins with less price-sensitive customers. However, by considering what might drive value for the customer by answering key questions—What needs aren't being met? How might those needs evolve or new ones emerge over time?—companies may uncover ways to increase loyalty and strengthen the customer relationship. For many in the workforce, focusing on value to others, rather than the tight prescriptions of faster or cheaper, also opens up space to work differently and be less transactional and more collaborative.

From the perspective of the workforce, people are afforded additional nonmonetary value when they are given opportunities to learn and develop new skills that will help them advance in their jobs, now and in the future. Consider the financial services company that made a deliberate decision not to aim for reductions in head count as it transformed its back-office finance and IT functions. Finance staff were given tools to automate and streamline much of their current work (data collection, metric calculation, report generation), and they were encouraged to use freed-up time to engage with the business partners they supported to identify more useful metrics and valuable insights to support decision making. At the same time, the customer-facing workers were trained to be better at understanding customers and finding ways to better serve them over time.

These steps led to major shifts: The company changed sales targets, shifted retail staff from pushing products to building customer relationships, and equipped loan officers with tablets so that they could serve customers remotely. By changing how they worked, rather than reducing jobs through automation, this organization created more engaging work for their employees. This approach allowed the organization to solve more interesting problems, which in turn led to better engagement than previous roles focused on routine reporting.

Meaning. This is an aspirational driver that seeks to support others in making a difference that matters and motivates people to continue to do better. How do we define this driver for companies? To start, it's about more than creating a qualitative mission statement or purpose. Also, it goes beyond corporate social responsibility and doesn't necessarily equate to doing something "good" or socially desirable. It starts by asking: What are the aspirations of our customers, employees, and partners?

As a future-of-work driver, *meaning* refers to connecting the work back to a deeper understanding of the participants involved—customers, workers, and other stakeholders—and the bigger impact the work will have on helping them achieve their aspirations. Wharton management professor Adam Grant found call-center employees were 171% more productive when they had the opportunity to spend time learning about the impact their services had on end customers. In this instance, the simple act of putting a face to the name helped create meaning in an otherwise routine job. At the same time, meaning also derives from the day-to-day work: Am I using my strengths and capabilities? Am I working with people I respect to deliver something of value?

Understanding and driving meaning is critical for companies because it is a key motivator and helps sustain effort over time. If you can articulate a purpose that matters across stakeholders, you will get an impact, but if you can also tap into the purpose and meaning for the workforce and connect to what matters for the customer, you'll get an amplifying effect. By seeking a better understanding of the underlying aspirations and sources of meaning for the customer, companies can also more effectively anticipate the evolving needs of the customer. The catch here is that meaning is more nuanced than cost or even value—it cannot easily be pushed. The individual worker or customer will ultimately decide if something is meaningful. The goal for business and talent leaders is to explicitly consider what meaning can be derived by customers and workers based on the design of products, services, and jobs, too.

The Imperative to Move Beyond Cost

Organizations are wired for short-term thinking with outsize focus on next-quarter results. Consequently, much of employees' attention and resources goes to incremental, efficiency-boosting activities. Given how few organizational leaders feel ready for the longer-term impact of the future of work, many continue to pursue reactive digital strategies—either executing a few visible but symbolic initiatives or bolting new technologies onto existing processes. For many organizations, these fragmented efforts leave much on the table—for their customers and workforce, as well as the company itself.

So, what can leaders who feel trapped in short-term approaches do? We recommend they begin by zooming out. Zooming out means focusing on the broader, long-term forces that are reshaping our global economy and providing a context for understanding how work is likely to evolve. Leaders can develop a shared understanding of how these forces are likely to affect their own markets over 10 to 20 years and a vision for how they will succeed in that future. This can help them look beyond the immediate, see the potential opportunity on the horizon, and set better strategies anchored in the long term. Considering the longer term can help pull us out of the narrow view that work is essentially static. This in turn allows us to rewire our thinking about near-term initiatives—What will help us develop the capabilities needed for the zoom-out vision?—without falling into a pattern of introducing incremental, reactive strategies. By utilizing the various dimensions outlined in the future-of-work drivers framework, leaders can help focus, and even accelerate, near-term initiatives to get much greater impact.

As market dynamics and the business environment become less stable and predictable, adopting this broader, more inclusive understanding of how cost, value, and meaning drive performance becomes an imperative. Those stuck in a cost focus will find diminishing returns with little upside, and the technologies defining the future of work will deliver one-off performance improvements. Ongoing cost reduction is an essential part of operational strategy, but as our and others' research shows, sustainable business value is primarily a function of market differentiation and revenue and market share growth.

The dynamic nature of the future requires us to move behind the one-size-fits-all approach to strategy and open our eyes to the possibilities of achieving aspirations that were otherwise impossible. Using the two dimensions of this framework, leaders have the potential to develop a broader perspective of the future of work that can help define near-term initiatives that will have greater impact. Further, they can avoid the risk of spreading resources too thinly across too many initiatives with only marginal impact.

There is no launch date for the future of work. Organizations must be fluid and flexible for adjusting to the current and future impacts of emerging technological and economic forces on the way we work, organize, and compete. However, by zooming out to gain a broader understanding of the opportunities ahead, leaders can better define the series of stages and initiatives that will make up the journey. Companies will glean more from the near-term initiatives they undertake, and leaders can make sense of the many activities and efforts underway. The future of work is human-driven, and it is up to us to set our sights on the future we want to create. So, to what end will you start designing the future of work in your organization?

The authors wish to acknowledge John Seely Brown for his contributions to this article.

15

It's Time to Rethink the
IT Talent Model

Will Poindexter and Steve Berez

Senior executives in the agile age know they have to recruit the best technical talent they can afford. Unfortunately, some of the best practices of former years have actually made it more difficult to hire the right people and increase the agility of the IT shop.

For example, as companies began to realize that their IT managers did not always see problems through a business lens, they brought in new ones with more business savvy. The new hires were good communicators, understood the connection between business priorities and technology, and managed relationships well throughout the rest of the organization. The problem was that many of them were not deep technologists. As these managers hired more like themselves, the technological skills of many companies suffered.

The unchecked use of external contractors has also contributed to the talent deficit. Some amount of labor sourcing is healthy, because it can help companies fill gaps quickly, acquire new skills, or take advantage of lower labor rates. But some companies shook this piggy bank too often to meet sudden increases in demand or dodge internal head count freezes. As internal talent spent more time managing contractors, their own technical skills atrophied. Contractors gained disproportionate control of intellectual property and innovations that could deliver a competitive advantage. How do you transform a technology organization when half the workers are not your employees?

Another problem has been in creating models in organizations for how products are built and maintained and who has accountability when things go wrong. Companies have embraced a model of separating where things are built from where they are supported, because it allows them to farm out maintenance and support to third parties. But whom do you call when something doesn't work or breaks in the middle of the night: the people who wrote the code or those who are responsible for supporting it?

To fix these problems, technology organizations need to strengthen their technical skills, reduce dependency on contractors, and expand accountability. Today, most technology organizations have three types of roles: watchers, doers, and thinkers. But as the future of IT takes shape, these roles must evolve. The watchers in particular—project managers, business analysts, relationship and resource managers—will need to find new ways to contribute. Wider adoption of agile and new ways of working will mean streamlined overhead, greater accountability and transparency, and less need for translators between business and technical staff.

What does the emerging talent model for IT entail? It draws on these principles:

Bring in the Engineering Manager

In agile organizations, supplanting the business-oriented IT manager is a true engineering manager, with the technical chops to check others' code but also enough business savvy to work closely with product managers and business owners. The engineering manager helps rebuild the technical credibility and prowess required to attract top-notch engineering talent—both experienced hires and campus recruits.

Retool the Watchers

The emerging talent model calls for more doers overall. So identify the watchers in your ranks who could be retrained into roles that add more of that kind of value. For example, project managers open to change could become scrum masters, and some business analysts could grow into product managers.

Unfortunately, there are often more watchers in an organization than there are new roles, given how much more efficient and effective operations are when you empower teams, give them accountability, and remove unnecessary bureaucracy. As a result, you might not be able to redeploy everyone.

Democratize Accountability

Doers are now taking on broader roles. For example, in most cases, product management is expanding to include both development and support, so those activities must be integrated by people who understand both.

When development managers at one of our client companies asked, "How many times do you think our top developers are going to receive calls in the middle of the night for production issues before they leave?" the CIO responded, "I don't know. How many times will we need to call and wake them up before they start writing better code?" As these developers came under pressure to deliver more functionality, reliability had suffered. So they were given responsibility for both. They didn't quit, as the manager had feared, but instead worked to improve the reliability because they had greater ownership for product outcomes. In parallel, these same developers work alongside the operations team to streamline integration and deployment of code, decreasing time to market while reducing defects.

Reduce Dependence on Contractors

Software innovation needs to come from employees. This means triaging different kinds of work and building agile teams that combine the right mix of internal and external talent. Of course, the goal is not to blindly cut contractors in pursuit of an artificial ratio. Companies should be smart about where they want to go and think critically about which mix will get them there as they marshal resources across technology management and recruiting.

Target tackled several of these challenges as it transformed its IT shop. It found that traditional recruiting efforts were not bringing in the engineering talent the company needed to move quickly in its market. The company's dependence on contractors for technical talent had limited its visibility as an employer of choice within software engineering communities. To put itself back on the map, Target embraced open-source technology (many of the strongest developers prefer it over proprietary code) and publicized its ambitions to transform and scale its digital technology. These moves helped attract and retain scarce engineering talent and reduce the company's dependence on third parties.

Agile is a powerful approach to delivering value. But on its own, it's not enough, and many organizations struggle to reap the benefits. Closing gaps in technical talent is critical to success—and doing so requires sustained commitment and attention from both business and technology leaders. Eventually, that may seem as obvious to most companies as aligning business and technology priorities is today. We aren't quite there yet.

16

New Ways to Gauge Talent and Potential

Josh Bersin and Tomas Chamorro-Premuzic

Most businesses understand that they must attract star performers—and compete fiercely for them—to thrive in the marketplace. What they struggle with is how to do it well. The perennial challenge of finding the right people and matching them with the right roles has become even more complex now that AI and robotics are rapidly changing jobs and in-demand technical skills are in short supply. While most organizations still rely on traditional hiring methods such as résumé screenings, job interviews, and psychometric tests, a new generation of assessment tools is quickly gaining traction and, we argue, making talent identification more precise and less biased.

Certain things have remained constant and are unlikely to change anytime soon. When sizing up candidates, managers try to predict job performance while assessing cultural fit and capacity to grow. Studies show that managers look for three basic traits: ability, which includes technical expertise and learning potential; likability, or people skills; and drive, which amounts to ambition and work ethic.[1]

What we need from talent identification tools and methods—old or new—has also stayed the same. To assess their effectiveness, we must look for a strong correlation between candidates' scores and subsequent job performance. This may sound obvious, but we've found in our work with recruiters and hiring managers that many of them use tools based instead on ease and familiarity—and rarely correlate them to results.

Emerging assessment methods can be grouped into three broad categories: gamified assessments, digital interviews, and candidate data mining. What they have in common is their ability to detect new talent signals (that is, new indicators of performance potential).[2] Here we'll explain how each of these methods work and their strengths and limitations.

Gamified Assessments

A new breed of psychometric tests for recruitment focuses on enhancing the candidate experience. These tools apply game-like features, such as real-time feedback, interactive and immersive scenarios, and shorter modules, which make the test-taking more enjoyable. The catch is that users' choices and behaviors are mined by computer-generated algorithms to identify suitability for a given role.

For example, HireVue's MindX employs gamified cognitive-ability tests by asking users to play sleek games—think Nintendo's Brain Age—that predict IQ. Pymetrics has done something similar with classic psychological tests such as the Balloon Analogue Risk Task, which evaluates candidates' impulsivity and risk-taking by examining how far they allow self-inflating balloons to expand before they burst (bigger balloons mean more rewards, but there are no rewards if they burst).

Arctic Shores, which is often used for evaluating college graduates, puts candidates through what feels like a series of 1990s arcade games and correlates their choices to standard personality traits and competencies. As these types of tools are used more widely in high-volume hiring environments, tool providers gather enough data to demonstrate significant links between candidates' scores on the games and their job performance.[3]

In addition, many companies are designing their own gamified assessments, which they position at the interface between hiring and marketing. For instance, Red Bull's Wingfinder is available to the general public and used to attract candidates through the drink company's social media channels. Candidates are provided an extensive report on their strengths and weaknesses, regardless of whether they are formally considered for a position.

Despite the branding and marketing benefits of gamification, as well as the obvious appeal of providing a more enjoyable assessment experience—which can result in a larger number of candidates—this approach to talent identification has two disadvantages. First, there is a natural tension between fun and accuracy. The more interesting and enjoyable the assessment experience, the less predictive it tends to be, not least because getting a comprehensive picture of a candidate's background requires longer testing time, and time is the enemy of fun. Second, to deliver a "cool" assessment experience, particularly if it is branded and comparable to some of the games people play purely for fun, the costs will increase significantly. It is one thing to design a standard Q&A type of self-report and another to create immersive game-like experiences for candidates—and talent acquisition budgets are generally quite limited when it comes to assessment tools.

Digital Interviews

The second major development in talent identification is the widespread use of digital interviews. On the surface, these tools look like any other videoconferencing technology, but they provide a couple of added advantages.

For one thing, interviewers or hiring managers can post their questions on the platform to create a structured (consistent and repeatable) interview protocol for stakeholders to use in their conversations with candidates, which helps them make fair, accurate comparisons. For another, algorithms can be used to flag and interpret relevant talent signals (facial expressions,[4] tone of voice, emotions[5] such as anxiety and excitement, language, speed, focus, and so on), replacing human observations and intuitive inferences with data-driven sorting and ranking.

Research has long suggested that job interviews are most predictive when they are highly standardized—that is, when they put all interviewees through the same process and have a predefined scoring key to make sense of the answers. Given that insight, video interviews can increase the accuracy of the job interview findings while reducing costs and enabling hiring organizations to operate at scale (in our conversations with HR executives, we've learned that companies such as JP Morgan Chase and Walmart do thousands of video interviews each year).

One question about such platforms is their tendency to replicate and reinforce biases that are inherent to any interviewing process. That's certainly a limitation. If the people responsible for making hiring decisions are themselves biased, we should not expect AI to erase that problem. To complicate matters further, if those same people are then tasked with evaluating new hires' performance, their biases will be masked. From a statistical standpoint, they may have correctly predicted future performance with their candidate selections—but to an extent, that prophecy is self-fulfilling.

Clearly, if you're making biased decisions about which outcomes to measure to gauge performance, that won't change with machine-learning models (though you will get faster results). One way to address this issue is by focusing less on individual traits, for instance, and more on group outcomes such as productivity numbers and revenues. For managers, 360-degree reviews can also be useful, because they crowdsource performance evaluations, mitigating individual biases. Another option is to "train" algorithms to ignore the signals that predict human bias but not job performance (such as gender, age, social class, and race). Tool providers like HireVue tell us they are doing this to eliminate the impact of skin color on hiring decisions, for example.

Candidate Data Mining

The third new approach, passively mining candidate data and analyzing people's digital footprints, is fast-growing as well. While it has mostly been used to serve up targeted consumer messages in marketing and advertising, it is equally applicable to talent identification in HR. Online behavior can reveal information about individuals' interests, personalities, and abilities, which in turn predicts their suitability for particular jobs or careers. For example, many hiring managers now investigate candidates' reputation, followership, and level of authority on networking websites such as LinkedIn and Facebook, and they use that information to rate and rank people. LinkedIn and Entelo provide tools that do this automatically for recruiters, by giving them a range of scores to help evaluate candidates.

While there is a big difference between popularity metrics and actual potential, networking sites represent true peer feedback, so recruiters find them very predictive.

Passive data scraping has been extensively examined in studies highlighting consistent links between people's social media activity and key job-related qualities.[6] For example, a team of researchers showed reliable connections between the groups people like on Facebook and their broad character traits, such as whether they are more or less extroverted or agreeable.[7] Given that these traits have been systematically associated with strong performance across different jobs, the findings suggest that Facebook data can provide useful information to employers about a person's potential fit for a job or role. Furthermore, the very character traits extracted from Facebook behavior and other social media signals—such as the words people use on Twitter or in blogs or emails—are markers for abilities, likability, and drive.

There's a dark side to this capability, though, because it exposes candidates' personal lives to intense scrutiny (particularly those in the Generation Z cohort, many of whom have been using social media practically since birth). Organizations must think about how they'll respect people's privacy while getting the information they need to make smart hiring choices. Even if the boundaries between private and public life have eroded, it is ethical to ensure that people are aware of how their data is used.

The Ethics of Talent Identification

Of course, it is essential that any tools for talent assessment and recruitment meet ethical guidelines. Although legal regulations, such as the EU's General Data Protection Regulation, are

The character traits
extracted from
candidates' social
media behavior are
markers for their
abilities, likability,
and drive.

context—and especially market—dependent, two basic considerations are critical across the board.

Promoting consent and awareness: There is now quite a big difference between what candidates believe employers know about
them and what employers really know—and hiring organizations have an ethical obligation to do what they can to close that
gap. Do candidates opt in to all parts of the talent identification
process? Do they understand what is being done with their data?
Do they have opportunities to provide or withhold consent for
the data being mined? If employers (and tool providers) aren't
transparent throughout the process, their brands could suffer
tremendous harm.

Fostering fairness: It's also important to consider the degree to
which hiring tools may stack the deck against certain groups of
candidates, particularly people of color, women, and individuals at a socioeconomic disadvantage. This has long represented
a problem for talent identification, but scientifically defensi-
ble assessment tools (like thoroughly validated psychometric
tests) go to great lengths to increase predictive accuracy while
reducing the risks of discrimination.[8] Newer tools and methods
must be scrutinized with the same lens. For example, video or
speech signals identified as markers of talent can also reflect
social class and educational background; selecting people based
on such signals may result in a more homogeneous workforce.
Organizations should be aware it is possible to make merito-
cratic hiring decisions that undermine social fairness, because
the best candidates on paper may also be the most privileged
candidates—those who enjoyed an elite education and benefit
from expansive networks.

Millions of people look into changing jobs every year—and employers must evaluate those candidates. As new tools for assessing talent become more mature, their costs decrease, and more companies can adopt them to improve the process and the yield of good hires.

Are organizations ready to use these tools effectively and responsibly? We think so, as long as HR and business leaders spend time carefully evaluating the issues raised here.

Hiring the right person is probably the most important decision a manager makes. If machines can make this process more accurate and less biased, every business can see tremendous benefits.

17

Pioneering Approaches to Re-skilling and Upskilling

Lynda Gratton

In the new world of work, we may not know for sure which jobs will be destroyed and what will be created, but one thing is clear: Everyone, whatever their age, will at some point have to spend time either re-skilling (learning new skills for a new position) or upskilling (learning current tasks more deeply). In every job, workers will have new technologies to learn and new personal relationships to navigate as those roles fit and refit into a changing economic landscape.

Embracing this idea requires a real sense of agency on the part of individuals. Each of us needs to be both motivated and prepared to put in the effort toward making learning a lifetime priority.

That's a good first step, but it will work only if corporations step up to make it possible.

The challenge is that old-style notions of training are far too slow and relatively expensive. They're often classroom-based and instructor-led. They're usually focused only on current employees, ignoring potential recruits.

Look around, though, and you'll see experiments and early pilots underway. Some companies are figuring out smart ways to engage on this issue—to the advantage of both individuals and the businesses themselves. Here are three pioneering examples that, although different in their approaches, together begin to set the scene for what could become a full-scale transformation.

Re-skilling in Unexpected Places

The leadership team at Microsoft has made it a significant business imperative to expand the provision of the company's cloud services. Making this a reality has meant building data centers in places both populous, like Dublin, Ireland, and remote, like Boydton, Virginia (population about 400), and Des Moines, Iowa (just over 200,000). The crucial job skills for these new locations are in data center management, with particular responsibilities in systems administration and troubleshooting.

These are tough skills to recruit for, and they're unlikely to exist in the smaller local populations in which some of these centers are based. What's more, few current Microsoft employees want to relocate to data locations like these. When they do, the retention rates tend to be poor.

The Microsoft team embraced this challenge by expanding its view of who could do these jobs and deciding to help create new pools of talent in each local community. Portia Wu, Microsoft's managing director of US public policy, told me that the key has been to bring different stakeholders together. For instance, for the Boydton and Des Moines locations, the company has worked with local community colleges in southern Virginia and Iowa to create new Microsoft Data Center Academies (DCAs). These schools train students to work in Microsoft facilities and other businesses with similar IT needs. Students have been supported by more than $315,000 in Microsoft scholarships.

Each DCA has run programs with cohorts of between 15 and 20 students, and to date more than 200 students have graduated. Some joined Microsoft, while others took their skills to related companies, helping to grow the overall technology environment in these regions.

Upskilling Using Technology

Deepening existing skills in new ways is often required when the routine tasks of a job become automated.

This is what has occurred, for example, in the role of the bank teller: Many tellers today are using some of their freed-up time to become more active ambassadors for the bank, gently cross-selling customers by suggesting other bank products. This "human" part of the job requires high levels of interpersonal skills such as empathy, listening, and judgment.

These are fiendishly difficult skills to develop at scale. Unlike many cognitive skills, social skills cannot be learned in a rule-based way—there is no specifiable path to social effectiveness. Building job-related social skills for a work environment requires an immersive learning experience, rehearsed in situations as close as possible to the real job, with lots of opportunities for practice. This kind of skill development is essentially a process of trial and error, where we behave in a certain way, get feedback through subtle social cues, and try again. Practice creates the muscle of habit.

It is this complexity that has dogged efforts to scale upskilling. But new pilots demonstrate that this sort of wide-scale training is possible. These training programs don't rely on expensive, classroom-based coaching, using instead a combination of virtual reality, artificial intelligence, and human trainers.

The technology learning group Mursion, for instance, helps develop complex human skills such as empathy by giving people in training a chance to listen to and interact with a difficult customer or employee. It's a classic training process—but in this case, the difficult customer or employee is a virtual-reality avatar. CEO Mark Atkinson told me that his company's design team has figured out how to simulate a stressful working environment in such a plausible way that it fools the brain into believing the VR experience is real.

Trainees are given a scenario such as facilitating a conversation to hear all sides and help a difficult employee interact better with colleagues. Trainees are encouraged to practice across a number of contexts, trying out different tactics with an avatar who responds back in an AI-driven conversation. They receive feedback and measure their progress in creating the fluency of conversation that is so crucial to high-level social skills.

Corporations have begun using this training at scale. The US-based hotel company Best Western International, for instance, used the Mursion system to upskill more than 35,000 employees in how to better express empathy for customers and take the initiative to immediately solve customer problems.

Leveraging the Wisdom of Age

The deep, tacit knowledge of how to perform a task is often held in the minds of experienced workers in what is termed *crystalline intelligence*. Many organizations see the value of capturing this knowledge and passing it on—but coaching time is often in short supply.

This was the challenge for the US telecom company Verizon. Its field-based technicians are called upon to support both new equipment and legacy technologies, such as the use of copper wire to transmit communications signals. Though older systems are declining in use, there is a crucial transition period before these legacy technologies become obsolete.

For Michael Sunderman, Verizon's executive director of global learning and development, one of the ways forward was to create trials that use the tacit knowledge of older current and retired subject matter experts to provide instruction to field-based technicians. This upskilling was particularly crucial when technicians encountered problems with legacy technologies unfamiliar to them.

In some cases, the experts worked with the technicians in the field, but geographic dispersion of expertise is increasingly a challenge—so the link between the two is now often virtual. While virtual communication via telephone, emails, and chat rooms has been important, in some cases it was not enough.

Sunderman told me that he and his team have partnered with augmented reality technology companies to develop new equipment and software tools that supplement the conversation. For example, some field technicians are equipped with augmented reality goggles that enable their office-based expert coaches to see what the technician sees in the field. The experts can then talk technicians through the solutions, assisting them in real time to become more skilled in the older technologies.

There is much we can learn from these three examples. They show the real benefits of thinking creatively about these challenges while considering them from a wider systems perspective. This creativity is crucial if we are to support the many millions of people around the world who will rely on upskilling or re-skilling to remain productive.

18

How Managers Can Best Support a Gig Workforce

Adam Roseman

IPOs from big tech companies like Uber, Lyft, Postmates, and DoorDash won't just draw attention and funds from investors on Wall Street. The disclosures these companies provide are likely to bring new scrutiny to how they—and, by extension, the gig economy in general—manage workers.

Already, some members of Congress are looking to step up protections for workers who try to cobble together a living through contingent and alternative arrangements. As Democratic Senator Mark Warner of Virginia said when reintroducing legislation in February 2019, "Changes in the nature of work mean that Americans are more likely to change jobs and be engaged in nontraditional forms of work than they were a generation ago,"[1] but federal policies have not evolved along with these economic shifts.

Having cofounded an app, Steady, to help people find sources of income in this economy, I see every day just how badly many workers are struggling. More than 4 million Americans are working part time for economic reasons, meaning they could not find full-time work or have received reduced hours due to economic slack.

Even among those who get enough hours to work full time, most don't receive benefits. And if they lose their jobs, most gig workers cannot collect unemployment.

This problem is only going to grow. A 2017 NPR/Marist poll found that 1 in 5 jobs is held by a worker under contract and that within a decade, contractors and freelancers could make up half the workforce.

It isn't just the workers who lose out due to this lack of stability. When people are grappling with financial stress, their health and productivity suffer. That stress is rampant among workers in general; 78% of US workers live paycheck to paycheck, and nearly 40% have a side hustle.

But the unpredictability gig workers can face, with income often varying month to month, can make their plight even worse.

To help workers with contingent or alternative arrangements in any industry, from sales to construction, here are three important steps managers can take.

Schedule at least two weeks out. Companies that allow people to work any time, like Instacart or TaskRabbit, get a lot of attention. But most of the jobs in the gig economy don't have this kind of flexibility. According to one study, 1099 workers are most plentiful in professions like agriculture, manufacturing, and childcare.

Far too often, these workers don't receive their schedules until just the day before they're needed. It becomes impossible for them to stitch together multiple jobs and make enough money to support themselves. Many can't simply supplement their incomes with app-based work whenever they're available, since they don't have access to a vehicle or they live in areas with limited demand for drivers and deliverers.

When managers provide workers with their schedules at least two weeks in advance, they empower workers to plan—and help them make a living.

Provide training. Career pathways are generally designed for full-time employees. They can see the next promotion to aim for and can parlay their experiences at one company into a full-time position at another. But gig workers often have a harder time building toward long-term careers.

This is especially true with workplaces that are experiencing rapid change. While people in traditional employment often receive training in new skills, tools, and technologies, contractors are left out. As other research on contingent workers has noted, "Rather than benefiting from the traditional route of gaining knowledge and training through the workplace, alternative workers tend to switch from job to job, losing access to professional development and advancement opportunities."[2]

By extending education and training opportunities to gig workers, managers can help them compete in the years ahead. The National Retail Federation Foundation is doing this through a program called RISE Up, helping to "build the retail industry's next generation of talent."

Offer loans. Four in 10 Americans couldn't cover an unexpected $400 expense without selling something or borrowing the money. More than one-quarter are skipping necessary medical care because they can't afford it. These and other findings from the Federal Reserve present a powerful reminder of the stress workers are under.

One helpful step business can take is to make loans available. Managers provide these in relatively small increments to employees when they face emergencies. Some companies have already begun doing this, while others are allowing paycheck advances. And some are making financial planning resources available to employees. Providing such benefits not just to full-time employees in traditional arrangements, but also to gig workers, can help alleviate stress.

To create stability for today's workforce, the United States needs a series of laws that will empower gig workers with basics like minimum wages and access to affordable health care. Some cities and states (like California) are already taking actions to protect workers. But businesses must help lead the way. And those that do—for instance, perhaps, Amazon, which raised its minimum wage to $15—stand to gain with happier, healthier workers who want to be a productive part of the team.

19

Unleashing Innovation with Collaboration Platforms

Massimo Magni and Likoebe Maruping

In business, difficult problems mean companies need diverse expertise to innovate and problem solve. Take the biomedical engineering company EpiBone. Facing complex problems such as bone reconstruction and implantation, the company relies on knowledge from a diverse disciplinary team of scientists, engineers, clinicians, and entrepreneurs. CEO Nina Tandon describes how this diverse collaboration has put the company at the frontier of bone reconstruction: "We take two things from the patient: a tridimensional X-ray and a sample of fat tissue so that we can extract stem cells out of it. We use these stem cells to fabricate a living bone on the basis of the data coming from the X-ray. After three weeks, we have a bone ready for implantation."

Businesses guided by a similar imperative to innovate can also leverage diverse expertise, but their teams often face the challenge of geographical distribution. Recent research conducted by Gartner states that over 50% of team communication occurs through collaboration platforms.

Based on projected market values, collaboration software revenues are expected to grow by 40% between 2015 and 2022. Demand for collaboration platforms is already at an all-time high, particularly with the proliferation of SaaS-based subscription models. Established incumbents such as Microsoft (Teams), Cisco (Spark), and Facebook (Workplace) all compete in the team-collaboration platform space. As the race to support team innovation rages on, businesses should focus more on how their distributed teams orchestrate collaboration and the conditions team leaders create. The specific collaboration platforms they choose are less important.

We conducted a study of over 600 team members, team coordinators, and managers who use collaboration platforms. Team members filled out an online survey, rating the effectiveness of the collaboration platform for supporting team interactions, and assessing leadership behaviors of team coordinators. Team coordinators were given a questionnaire about their team's ability to integrate knowledge, and team supervisors were surveyed on team innovation success.

Our results suggest there are two key factors or challenges that affect how much of a benefit teams get from collaboration platforms. The first factor is how well the collaboration platform supports activities needed to integrate team knowledge, despite geographically different locations. The second is whether team leaders can establish conditions that foster knowledge integration in a digital environment.

Ideal Collaboration Platforms

In organizations, success for teams requires fitting different individual knowledge bases and perspectives to particular problems and opportunities. Attempting to do this through a collaboration platform involves many considerations. Our analysis of survey data, corroborated with experiences shared during informal interactions with participants, shows that ideal collaboration platforms enable knowledge integration, and therefore team innovation, by supporting three main aspects of teamwork: preparation, execution, and well-being.

Enable team preparation. Orchestrating the integration of diverse knowledge for innovation means teams need to set the stage for coordinated action. This need is particularly acute for distributed teams, because they cannot observe each other's behavior beyond what happens on the collaboration platform. They also don't have the advantage of understanding each other's availability and needs, enjoyed by teams working in a single location.

Setting the stage entails reaching a common understanding of the team's mission (what is our charge?), establishing team goals (what innovation outcome are we attempting to achieve?), defining team members' roles and responsibilities (who is responsible for what in this innovation process?), and formulating a strategy to achieve the innovative outcome (how do we get there?).

We found teams were better prepared to integrate diverse knowledge when the collaboration platform allowed them to document their mission and goals, roles, and responsibilities, and create a process road map. Team members could access and revisit these documents on the go at their convenience. Having access to these documents gave more meaning to the independent actions taken by members who were subject matter experts in different knowledge domains. It also let them see the forest for the trees.

For example, one participant in the study underscored the importance of working with a collaboration platform that allows team members to have an immediate picture of who is responsible for what, and how each member fits with the overall goal. When team members are distributed across different geographical locations, they need to know each member's role in the overall plan. Otherwise, you risk having team members rowing at 120% but in different directions.

Empower complex execution. Setting the stage is not enough. Complex problems, diverse experts, and a variety of information formats can complicate the process of collaboration. Platforms supporting a great breadth of media forms give teams more options. Knowledge can be exchanged and integrated via text, audio, video, images, virtual 3D environments, and shared whiteboards, among others. Our research shows that collaboration platforms supporting multiple formats gives teams the flexibility they need.

Team members also need to be able to coordinate their activities in terms of sequencing deliverables, evaluating results, and tracking progress. When platform technology does not support these activities, team members may tend to focus on their own local goals and overlook the team's objectives. Teams need collaboration platforms that let them determine the availability of team members in real time, receive status updates when deliverables have been shared, and track how deliverables contribute to achieving key milestones in the innovation process.

Shared digital workspaces, combined with digital archives of the group's work, should also allow team members to back each other up if the need arises. When problems emerge, teams may not be able to wait for unavailable members, especially when working across different locations and time zones. In one team we analyzed, a member noted the importance of being able to support team coordination by providing constant updates on who is doing what on the platform. They indicated that this real-time awareness of each member's progress presented opportunities to course correct, whether to reassign tasks or reassess priorities and deadlines. This transparency allowed team members to respond immediately to unanticipated problems, and other team members could be made aware of actions taken to solve the issue.

Facilitate well-being. Collaboration is a human endeavor, and digital environments can be fraught with potential minefields that can derail a team's innovation efforts. Innovation itself is difficult because there are no predefined solutions. This can lead to tensions and frustrations when teams face major headwinds. Teams composed of members with diverse expertise inherently bring different perspectives and understandings of problems and possible solutions—which can easily lead to conflict. Finally, work in digital spaces can be isolating, leading members to feel disconnected from social interactions.

Failure to empower team members to openly share their points of view can build resentment and leave members feeling like their ideas are not valued. Our study showed that team members are more likely to engage with each other to resolve impasses and misunderstandings when they feel the collaboration platform supports expressive communication forms. As an example, one member noted that emails are usually a source of conflict because of the misunderstandings that may emerge through written text when face-to-face interaction is lacking.

Collaboration platforms that afford members a unified workspace to discuss, share opinions, and work jointly can be seen as the digital "watercooler." Team members need visibility into all ongoing discussions and interactions so they don't feel left out.

Leading People, Not Platforms

Giving distributed teams of experts a digital collaboration platform doesn't always mean success. It's common for leadership to focus on enforcing use of the tool, given the investment an organization might make in acquiring a collaboration platform. However, our study suggests that leaders cannot stop at simply implementing a collaboration platform. They must play a central role in enabling innovation by providing a vision of the future and nurturing a climate of fairness, where team members can express their views and treat each other with respect.

Leaders need to ignite inspiration in their team by setting the vision for what the innovation will achieve and inspiring them to make the most of their diverse expertise. Our study shows that inspirational messages from leadership reinforces team members' willingness to try new problem-solving approaches. Such messages also encourage them to innovate through continuous recombination of their expertise.

When leaders promote an atmosphere of fairness, team members feel empowered to provide and request feedback, even if they are physically isolated and have little visibility into interactions that might occur off-platform. Leaders should ensure transparency about how decisions are made within the team and encourage team members to have accountability for their interactions—such transparency will guarantee nobody feels left out in the innovation process.

As with many user-facing technology decisions, managers and team leaders need to consider both the complexities of the work being done and the people doing that work. In making these decisions, leaders need to shift their emphasis to people utilizing these collaboration platforms.

The key to achieving innovation success through collaboration platforms—make it about the people—not the technology.

IV

Case Study

20

Rebooting Work for a Digital Era: How IBM Reimagined Talent and Performance Management

David Kiron and Barbara Spindel

Note: The research and analysis for this case study was conducted under the direction of the authors as part of an *MIT Sloan Management Review* research initiative in collaboration with and sponsored by McKinsey & Company.

Until recently, IBM's performance management system followed a traditional approach that revolved around yearlong cycles, ratings, and annual reviews. This case study explores how, after recognizing that the model was holding back the organization, IBM reimagined its performance management system with a model that favors speed and innovation and cultivates a high-performance culture.

Introduction

In 2015, IBM was in the midst of a tremendous business transformation. Its revenue model had been disrupted by new technology and was shifting toward artificial intelligence and hybrid cloud services. To increase its rate and pace of innovation, the company was rapidly changing its approach to getting work done. New, agile ways of working together with new workforce skills were required to accomplish its portfolio shift. But standing in the way was an outdated performance management (PM) system employees did not trust. Diane Gherson, chief human resources officer and senior vice president of human resources, recognized that IBM's approach to performance management would need to be entirely reimagined before the organization could fully engage its people in the business transformation.

Gherson says the performance management system then in place followed a traditional approach, one that revolved around a yearlong cycle and relied on ratings and annual reviews. "You'd write in all your goals at the beginning of the year, and at the end of the year, your manager would give you feedback and write a short blurb and then give you your rating," she says.

That approach was "holding us back," Gherson says. "The massive transformation meant we were shifting pretty dramatically into new spaces and doing work really differently. Whereas efficiency was very important in the prior business model, innovation and speed had become really important in the new business model. And when you're trying to make that kind of a fundamental shift, it's important, obviously, to bring your employees along with you."

Gherson knew from employee roundtables and surveys that IBMers didn't have confidence or trust in the existing PM system. This view was at odds with the views of other senior leaders, who felt the system in place was working well from their perspective.

It took Gherson more than a year to convince her peers in senior leadership that IBM's digital transformation would not succeed without higher levels of employee engagement, and that meant focusing on the existing PM system. Eventually she won them over. As for the traditional PM system that was holding

IBM's approach
to performance
management would
need to be entirely
reimagined before
the organization
could fully engage its
people in the business
transformation.

the company back? "We threw all that out," Gherson says. "We kept our principle of cultivating a high-performance culture, but pretty much everything else changed."

Company Background

The year 2015 was hardly the first time the company had found itself in the midst of a fundamental shift. IBM has had to reinvent itself time and again to remain relevant. Founded in 1911 as machinery manufacturer Computing-Tabulating-Recording Company, IBM over the decades has repeatedly adjusted its business focus—from early data processing to PC hardware to services to software systems—in response to evolving markets and competitive pressures.

Today, IBM, headquartered in Armonk, New York, employs about 360,000 people in 170 countries. After 22 consecutive quarters of declining revenue, the company reversed the trend in the fourth quarter of 2017 and subsequently has shown revenue growth. Growth in its cloud, artificial intelligence, cybersecurity services, and blockchain units have contributed to the turnaround, with about half of its revenues now derived from new business areas. Indeed, these days, IBM is betting big on AI and hybrid cloud, recently announcing plans to acquire open-source software pioneer Red Hat, an innovator of hybrid cloud technology, for $34 billion. With that notable acquisition, the company is making a bold bid to compete against heavyweights like Google, Amazon, and Microsoft in the cloud services market.

The new strategic direction has necessitated a change in how IBM's talent is managed and how the work of the digital enterprise is done. "In a classic, traditional model, a manager will oversee the work of an employee and, therefore, have firsthand knowledge of how they're doing," Gherson observes. "That traditional model is long gone in most companies. Work is more fluid."

At IBM, work is being done differently in three fundamental ways. One is a stronger emphasis on project work: Individuals move around the organization to work on various projects and initiatives, joining teams for short stints before moving on to new teams to tackle new challenges. Two, the entire concept of performance is shifting from primarily emphasizing performance outcomes to a model that also emphasizes the "how," including the continuous development and application of new skills to keep up with the exponential rate of change in technology. Finally, with the adoption of agile ways of working, continuous feedback becomes a critical part of workflow. The new PM system needed to abandon the concept of an annual feedback event and find a way to reinforce a culture of feedback—up, down, and across.

Meanwhile, digital transformation in the economy at large is exerting pressure on IBM as the tech giant strives to maintain an edge over its competitors. As a result of these internal and external changes, the company has seen the need to prioritize not only innovation and agility but also the continual development of employee skills, since what it requires of its talent base has also changed, with the need to continually develop employee skills becoming paramount.

Test-Driving a New System

The company's key decision was to crowdsource its new performance management system rather than impose something top-down on its workforce, which was not consistent with agile methodologies or design thinking. Gherson says it was "really important to have employees feel like they were stakeholders in the new design, not just bystanders or consumers of it." To that end, IBM undertook a process for designing the system that was a radical departure from the past. "There were many skeptics initially," Gherson recalls, highlighting the challenges of the project. IBM relied heavily on enterprise design thinking, creating a minimum viable product (MVP), and invited the workforce to test it and offer feedback. Gherson likens the process to "giving people a concept car that they can drive and kick the tires as opposed to asking them what they would like to have in a car." The rollout was fast: The September 2015 launch of the MVP happened within a couple of months of the first design-thinking session.

While many employees were thrilled that the traditional approach to performance management was on its way out the door, most were skeptical that the replacement program would be an improvement. As Joanna Daly, IBM's vice president of

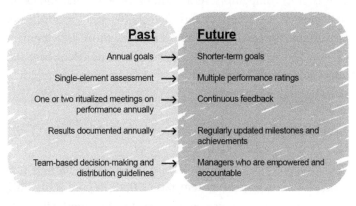

Past	Future
Annual goals $\longrightarrow$	Shorter-term goals
Single-element assessment $\longrightarrow$	Multiple performance ratings
One or two ritualized meetings on performance annually $\longrightarrow$	Continuous feedback
Results documented annually $\longrightarrow$	Regularly updated milestones and achievements
Team-based decision-making and distribution guidelines $\longrightarrow$	Managers who are empowered and accountable

Changes to IBM's Performance Management

The eventual result
was aligned to
the employees'
input, providing
a performance
management system
focused more on
feedback and less on
assessment.

compensation, benefits, and HR business development, recalls, "Employees actually said to us, 'We don't believe that you want our input. We think you already know what you're going to do, and you're just sort of pretending to ask for our input.' We had to figure out how to prove to employees that we were authentic and serious in wanting them to shape this."

HR did so in a simple way: by asking employees what they wanted, giving their responses due consideration, and playing back what it was hearing. "We asked, 'What do you want to get out of our approach to performance?'" Daly says. "And the answer we got was they wanted richer feedback. And they hated being defined by a single assessment rating."

When Gherson blogged about the new system on the company's internal platform, her first entry was viewed by 75,000 IBMers within hours, with 18,000 responding with detailed suggestions. The company used its proprietary Watson text analytics to sort through what employees wrote, enabling Gherson to put out a second blog within 48 hours enumerating which elements employees liked and which they disliked. The company proceeded through numerous iterations and playbacks, with employees continuously participating in the design process. Management even reached out personally to the most vocal critics at every step, directly engaging their input in producing the next prototype. The eventual result—officially launched in February 2016 and called Checkpoint—was aligned to the employees' input, providing a PM system focused more on feedback and less on assessment. (See "Changes to IBM's Performance Management" on page 162 for key differences between the old and new system.)

Rather than receiving a single rating at an annual review, employees now have more frequent check-ins with managers. Through the company's mobile ACE (appreciation, coaching, and evaluation) app, they also can seek feedback from peers, managers, or employees they manage.

The new and more agile system allows IBMers to revise their goals throughout the year. In response to crowdsourced input during the design process, employees are assessed according to their business results, impact on client success, innovation, personal responsibility to others, and skills. Managers are held accountable through pulse and mini-pulse surveys of the people they oversee, with poor results leading to training or, in some cases, removal from management.

Checkpoint is a far cry from the previous stand-alone HR program that rated and ranked employees. It's aligned to the critical factors for IBM's success and designed to ensure that the company achieves advantage with its talent in a fast-moving competitive landscape.

Checkpoint has been a major contributor to employee engagement, which has increased by 20% since IBM deployed the revitalized performance management system. In fact, in the company's annual engagement pulse survey, employees pointed to Checkpoint as the change that made the biggest difference in their experience at IBM.

Focus on Learning and Growing

Technological change—in the marketplace and in IBM's business focus—is driving an unremitting need for new skills, making their development an essential part of IBM's corporate strategy. "In today's world, skills are actually more important than jobs," Gherson declares. "In order to reinvent our company, we need everyone to reinvent their skills on a continuous basis. You can't hire someone because they have a particular skill. You have to hire someone because they have the capacity to continue to learn." To that end, in addition to the new approach to performance management, talent management at IBM now includes a personalized learning platform and a personalized digital career adviser.

The platforms use data to infer which skills employees have and connect them with learning to build those skills that are increasingly in demand. The personalized program is "really accessible, very consumer-friendly," Gherson says. "It has everything: internal and external courses, *Harvard Business Review* articles, *MIT Sloan Management Review* articles, YouTube videos—you name it. And it serves it up for you as an individual, based on your unique role. It will say, 'Given what you've taken so far and your career goals, here are some recommendations and here's what people like you have taken and how they've rated it.'"

To encourage career mobility, IBM launched a digital coach for employees wishing to advance their careers within the company. My Career Advisor (known commercially as Watson Career Coach) was created by employees during a companywide hackathon. It features a virtual assistant that uses data to provide personalized career counseling, such as average time to promotion from an employee's current role and career steps taken by others to acquire the job a user might want. Another related platform, Blue Matching, serves IBM employees internal job opportunities tailored to their qualifications and aspirations, inferred from their CVs.

What enables these learning and career programs, says Daly, is "having more data available and having better insights to guide the user. These new digital platforms mean we can get these insights directly into the hands of employees and their managers." Also essential has been uniting these platforms. "It's not about having a learning platform and having separately an internal jobs platform," Daly notes. "It's how do we integrate these two together with AI-enabled advice for employees to explore? What kind of job should I do next? What are my skills gaps if I want to pursue that job, and then what learning would I take to close that gap?"

Real-Time Insights

The new PM system was about agility and prioritizing feedback over assessment. IBM elected to go further and figure out how to use all the insights it was developing from its analytics and AI capabilities to ensure that useful insights could readily emerge and be accessible to both HR and the workforce.

"Thanks to these digital experiences, we've modernized how to deliver insights to our workforce and management—right when they need it," Daly says. She cites compensation decisions as an example. Using machine learning, "we advise managers about which employees should get the highest salary increase. We arrive at the recommendation using dozens of internal and external data sources. This helps with more transparent conversations between the manager and her employee," she says. "We give managers talent alerts directly on their personalized dashboard. For example, the system might observe, 'Hey, your team member has been in her band level for a few years and is a good performer and is building her skills. Have you thought about promoting her?'"

Going forward, Daly anticipates that more predictive and prescriptive insights will be transmitted directly to managers and employees at the moment they're needed most, embedded in the workflow.

Preventing Attrition

"In our industry, talent is the No. 1 issue," Gherson contends. "And so, it's really important that we attract and develop and continue to upgrade our skills and retain talent if we're going to win in this market." Despite more than 7,000 job applicants coming into IBM every day, with a tech talent shortage and ongoing talent wars in AI and cybersecurity, retention becomes particularly crucial; experts agree that in the coming decades, there won't be enough qualified people to fill available jobs.

Gherson and her team received a patent for their predictive attrition program, which was developed at IBM using Watson AI algorithms to predict which employees were likely flight risks. Most managers were initially skeptical at the notion that algorithms could have more insight into their employees' intentions than they did—until the algorithm consistently made correct predictions. Then, Gherson recalls, "We started getting these little notes from managers saying, 'How did you know?'"

Significantly, the technology is about prescription in addition to prediction. "We reach out to you as a manager," Gherson explains, "and we tell you that you've got someone who is at high risk to leave and here are the actions we recommend you take." Because the AI is able to infer which skills individual employees possess, it can then recommend actions for managers to implement—often related to furthering skills development—to prevent them from leaving. By helping their employees develop new skills, managers bolster employee engagement and increase job satisfaction, advantages in a talent-scarce market environment. "The attrition rate of the people we touch with this program is minuscule compared to the control group," Gherson

More predictive and prescriptive insights will be transmitted directly to managers and employees at the moment they're needed most, embedded in the workflow.

says, noting the improvement in employee retention has already saved IBM nearly $300 million.

The Evolving Role of HR

Given the heightened significance of talent, HR, as the function primarily responsible for talent, has a revitalized role to play in executing corporate strategy and driving value at IBM.

To achieve a more central role in value creation, IBM's HR function had to be freed from the tasks that traditionally consumed so much of its managers' time. "People have a million questions: 'When do I have to sign up for my 401(k)?' 'What's the deadline for the health benefits program enrollment?' These are all findable pieces of data, but actually finding them has always been the hardest part," Gherson says. "I wouldn't say that's the highest value that HR could provide, but it's a lot of what HR has been doing. Maybe in some companies that's all HR does. But that's not the purpose of HR. You don't need HR to answer those questions. You just need really great bots and virtual assistants."

Here, the company again exploited its own capabilities in AI and analytics. In HR alone, IBM currently deploys 15 virtual assistants and chatbots, and the company is diligent about measuring both employees' experience and the effectiveness of the bots in responding to questions. With the bots taking on routine tasks previously performed by people, IBM's HR function can devote itself to what Gherson sees as its real purpose: "to create competitive advantage with your talent and improve the employee experience."

Of course, technology and data are vital not just in freeing up the humans on the HR team but also in optimizing their performance. "For too long, HR people have relied on just being highly intuitive: 'I think this person's going to be a good fit for the job' or 'I think a two-year assignment is the right length,' or whatever," Gherson observes.

"And actually, you can employ science-based methods to come up with an estimate—for example, there's an 80% chance they'll fail in this job because they lack these capabilities or there's a 50% chance that you'll get no return on your investment in that international assignment because it's too short," she says. "So we should be able to give much better advice to the people that we support."

Gherson acknowledges that working this way also requires culture change within the HR function, which demands different skills like data science and different job roles to fully realize the disruption. She has invested in a robust re-skilling education program for her team of HR professionals.

Gherson says HR can't simply stop at using technology to detect patterns. Giving managers data on, say, turnover rate, without also offering guidance on how to use that information, leaves them to rely once again on intuition to solve problems. As with the predictive attrition program, IBM pairs reporting data with recommendations for action.

"Technology enables us to not just report, but to then say, 'If you keep doing what you're doing, here's what the picture will look like a month from now, a year from now. Your cost of labor will be higher than your competitors by 12% if you carry on hiring at the rate you're hiring. So here's a prediction that's going to be a bit of a wake-up call for you. But if you take these actions, here's the impact,'" Gherson explains.

"We're going from intuitive to reporting to predicting to prescribing," she adds. "And if we can take it all the way to that level, then we're really adding value. We're very proud of the fact that through these talent programs, HR delivered more than $107 million in benefits in the last year."

Conclusion

IBM's efforts to modernize its performance management system are part of an ongoing process. "We will continue to refine the measurement and expectations of skills growth in IBM as it becomes clear that we need to become a fabulous re-skilling-at-scale machine and hold ourselves accountable to that," Gherson says. Daly echoes that point: "These aren't programs that HR is developing. This is a new way of working that all IBMers are developing together so that we can keep our skills up to date as things keep changing in the future."

Commentary: HR Transformation as the Engine for Business Renewal

Anna A. Tavis

Industry disruptions have headlined business news since the early 2000s. With the cloud revolution driving change in global markets, traditional built-to-last companies have had to rapidly transform themselves to survive, adapt, and compete. Market-facing customer service, sales, and marketing functions reinvented themselves in the new digital image a decade ago. Although HR is a latecomer to the digital scene, it stands ready to undergo its own reinvention armed with smart technology, data-driven insights, and a renewed sense of purpose.

To paraphrase Diane Gherson, IBM's chief human resources officer, talent is unquestionably the new economy's No. 1 competitive asset. HR, as a traditional caretaker of talent, has to leapfrog generations of evolution, moving from intuition to reporting to predicting and ultimately to prescribing—all in a matter of a few years. Some companies, like IBM, are successfully making this leap. Critics, so ready to question HR's relevance and viability, should take note.

This case study describes HR transformation at IBM. It is particularly instructive for companies embarking on their own HR digital transformation efforts. IBM's most important lessons are less about the specific solutions they introduced and more about the way they went about finding their new philosophy and their new operating model. The IBM story is as much about what they decided not to do as it is about what they ended up doing.

Gherson's most consequential first step was to abandon the practice of benchmarking other companies and not to rely on HR experts to renew her strategy. She turned instead to IBM's own employees for answers. Not surprisingly, the message her team heard from employees was not always in line with the view of senior management, which did not believe much in HR could change. It became clear that IBM's transformation was to be anchored in agile ways of working. The company's traditional performance management (PM) was seen by employees, however, as an administrative chain holding back the adoption of fast agile ways of working. The decision was made to radically redesign PM with employee experience in mind. In the process, all other functional areas in HR were redesigned and realigned to serve HR's new purpose.

The following 10 decision points are worth considering when reviewing the IBM case in the context of your own organizational transformation:

1. **Decide where to start.** IBM's first and highest priority was to redesign its PM system. The team turned to its own employees for redesign ideas, not HR experts or senior leaders.

   What you can do: Identify the weakest link in your talent management system. If it's your PM approach, this is where change should begin.

2. **Connect your transformation to an existing element of your strategy.** IBM used its adoption of agile practices across the organization as the primary catalyst to overhaul its entire talent management system.

   What you can do: Choose the one key performance indicator (KPI) that intersects with talent that will have the most impact on your business.

3. **Renew your talent/HR purpose.** By committing to employee experience, engagement, and learning, IBM shifted away from an earlier focus on differentiation and high potentials.

   What you can do: Decide what type of culture you want to have. Assess how fast you can move from an administrative compliance- and appraisal-based approach to being employee-centric and learning-focused.

4. **Start with a broad impact.** Identify the most consequential first step with the broadest possible impact. IBM made a PM redesign the priority in its talent transformation process and had the capacity, capability, and political capital to go global with its minimum viable product (MVP) for the entire organization.

What you can do: Identify whether performance management is the weakest link in your talent management system and where the pain points are for your employees and management.

5. **Select the design method consistent with your new purpose.** For IBM, agility and design thinking became key methodologies HR successfully applied.

   What you can do: Select and agree on design principles and method(s) consistent with your talent philosophy and aligned with your purpose. Teach those skills and test to see if they work for all.

6. **Get your organization's buy-in to support your transformation effort.** IBM took a two-tiered approach to secure buy-in: (1) It earned employee trust and engagement by crowdsourcing design ideas from across the company, and (2) it won over senior management by running successful experiments proving that attrition could be predicted by data.

   What you can do: Learn to listen. Generate insights and communicate decisions supported by the evidence you collect. Engage key stakeholder groups with data relevant to them.

7. **Decide how to test and improve the designed product.** IBM went for speed, customer feedback, and continuous improvement. Having designed and released their crowdsourced PM process, Checkpoint, in record time, the company "proceeded through numerous iterations and playbacks, with employees continuously participating in the design process."

   What you can do: Choose one of three approaches:

   • Launch a companywide MVP. Your priority initiative is based on your company's KPIs and readiness for the companywide rollout.

- Experiment and create a proof of concept. Run a series of experiments starting with the business units most ready to innovate. Show results to others.
- A combination of the above two approaches.

8. **Go beyond performance management.** Decide on your next steps. Successful implementation of the redesigned PM process revealed further strategic talent needs for IBM:

   - Accelerate and personalize skills renewal.
   - Customize decision support for managers.
   - Create an internal marketplace for jobs.

   What you can do: PM renewal has a domino effect on all HR processes and tools. What comes next on the renewal list will have to be decided by your company depending on its strategic priorities. Meanwhile, HR will have to renew and upskill itself as the transformation process continues.

9. **Assess how to turn technology and data into the greatest enablers of transformation.** IBM HR fully leverages its tech and AI capabilities, often creating its own tech tools. My Career Advisor, for example, is IBM's mobile in-house career coach created by employees at a companywide hackathon. Blue Matching serves IBM employees with notice of new internal job opportunities tailored to their qualifications and aspirations.

   What you can do: Technology and automation are central to the transformation of HR. Yet no two companies' technological and data capabilities are alike. Choose your tools wisely, develop technical expertise internally, or borrow your experts. Do not overspend on systems unless you understand how they will deliver.

10. **Integrate tools, platforms, and processes with employee experience in mind.** IBM's case shows how to bring all pro-

cesses, tools, and platforms together into one renewed talent ecosystem. "It's not about having a learning platform and . . . an internal jobs platform," noted Joanna Daly, IBM's vice president of compensation, benefits, and HR business development; it's how they integrate together with AI-enabled advice for employees to explore what jobs they should do next.

What you can do: No matter where you decide to start, integration should be your final destination.

IBM's case could be the timely accelerator of your own company's HR transformation. There is a lot to learn here, but no one's "best practice" is a replacement for your own discovery. The best lesson to learn from Gherson and her team is their innovative attitude and openness to experiment in the face of the unknown. Learning to innovate, take on risks, and show courage is what IBM's HR has shown us how to do. It is now the right time to take the right lessons from IBM and apply them and scale. Best of luck as you begin.

Contributors

Carrie Altieri, Michael Fitzgerald, Jennifer Martin, Allison Ryder, Karina van Berkum

Acknowledgments

Joanna Daly, vice president, compensation, benefits, and HR business development, IBM

Diane Gherson, chief human resources officer and senior vice president, human resources, IBM

Contributors

Steve Berez is a partner with Bain & Company's Technology and Agile Innovation practices.

Ethan Bernstein is the Edward W. Conard Associate Professor of Business Administration at Harvard Business School.

Josh Bersin is a global industry analyst and the founder of Bersin by Deloitte.

Matthew Bidwell is an associate professor of management and faculty codirector of the Wharton People Analytics initiative at the University of Pennsylvania.

Ryan Bonnici is chief marketing officer of G2 Crowd and former director of global marketing at HubSpot.

Tomas Chamorro-Premuzic is the chief talent scientist at ManpowerGroup and a professor of business psychology at University College London and Columbia University.

Rob Cross is the Edward A. Madden Professor of Global Leadership at Babson College.

Chris DeBrusk is a partner in the financial services and digital practices of Oliver Wyman.

Federica De Stefano is a postdoctoral fellow of the Wharton People Analytics initiative at the University of Pennsylvania.

Thomas H. Davenport is the President's Distinguished Professor of IT and Management at Babson College, a fellow at the MIT Initiative on the Digital Economy, and a senior adviser to Deloitte's Analytics and Cognitive practices.

Angela Duckworth is the Christopher H. Browne Distinguished Professor of Psychology at the University of Pennsylvania and the founder and CEO of Character Lab.

Ken Favaro is the sole proprietor of act2, which advises CEOs, leadership teams, and boards on strategy, innovation, and organization.

Lynda Gratton is a professor of management practice at London Business School and director of the school's Human Resource Strategy in Transforming Companies program. She is coauthor of *The 100-Year Life: Living and Working in an Age of Longevity* (Bloomsbury, 2016).

Peter Gray is a professor at the McIntire School of Commerce at the University of Virginia.

Lindred (Lindy) Greer is an associate professor of management and organizations at the University of Michigan's Ross School of Business and faculty director at its Sanger Leadership Center.

John Hagel III is cochairman for Deloitte's Center for the Edge.

Manish Jhunjhunwala is the founder and CEO of Trefis, a data-manipulation technology and analytics provider.

David Kiron is editorial director at *MIT Sloan Management Review*.

Frieda Klotz is a freelance journalist and correspondent for *MIT Sloan Management Review*.

David Lazer is University Distinguished Professor of Political Science and Computer Sciences at Northeastern University and visiting scholar at the Institute for Quantitative Social Science at Harvard.

Massimo Magni is an associate professor in the Department of Management and Technology at Bocconi University, and professor of leadership and managerial development at SDA Bocconi School of Management.

Likoebe Maruping is an associate professor in the Department of Computer Information Systems in the J. Mack Robinson College of Business at Georgia State University.

Kelly Monahan is a research manager in Deloitte Services LP within Deloitte's Center for Integrated Research.

Will Poindexter is a partner with Bain & Company's Technology and Agile Innovation practices.

Reb Rebele is a senior research fellow for the Wharton People Analytics initiative at the University of Pennsylvania and a PhD candidate studying personality processes at the University of Melbourne in Australia.

Adam Roseman is cofounder and CEO of Steady.

Michael Schrage is a research fellow at the MIT Initiative on the Digital Economy.

Jeff Schwartz is the US Future of Work Leader at Deloitte Consulting.

Jesse Shore is assistant professor of information systems at Boston University's Questrom School of Business.

Brian Solis is principal analyst and futurist at Altimeter and author of *Lifescale: How to Live a More Creative, Productive, and Happy Life* (Wiley, 2019).

Barbara Spindel is a freelance writer and editor specializing in culture, history, and politics.

Anna A. Tavis is a clinical associate professor of human capital management and academic director of the human capital management program at New York University.

David Waller is a partner and the head of data science and analytics for Oliver Wyman Labs.

Adam Waytz is a psychologist and associate professor of management and organizations at the Kellogg School of Management at Northwestern University. His first book, *The Power of Human* (Norton, 2019), is about the importance of humanity in an increasingly humanless world.

Maggie Wooll is head of research at Deloitte's Center for the Edge.

Notes

Chapter 2

1. M. Arntz, T. Gregory, and U. Zierahn, "Revisiting the Risk of Automation," *Economics Letters* 159, no. C (October 2017): 157–160.

2. C. B. Frey and M. A. Osborne, "The Future of Employment: How Susceptible Are Jobs to Computerisation?" *Technological Forecasting and Social Change* 114 (January 2017): 254–280.

3. L. Alton, "How Should Millennials Prepare for the Coming Robotic Revolution?" *Forbes*, January 29, 2018, https://www.forbes.com/sites/larryalton/2018/01/29/how-should-millennials-prepare-for-the-coming-robotic-revolution/.

4. A. J. Gustein and J. Sviokla, "7 Skills That Aren't About to Be Automated," *Harvard Business Review*, July 17, 2018, https://hbr.org/2018/07/7-skills-that-arent-about-to-be-automated; A. Westervelt, "Robots Are Coming for Our Jobs: Here Are 5 Ways to Prepare," updated December 6, 2017, https://www.huffpost.com/entry/robots-jobs-automation-employment-training_n_5a0c3f77e4b0b17ffce184a1; M. Ford, "How We Can Best Prepare for Job Automation," *Forbes*, December 28, 2018, https://www.forbes.com/sites/quora/2018/12/28/how-we-can-best-prepare-for-job-automation; and C. C. Miller, "How to Prepare for an Automated Future," *New York Times*, May 3, 2017, https://nyti.ms/2pwDS4s.

5. S. Goldberg, "New Walgreens Program Blurs Lines between Pharmacy, Retail," *Crain's Chicago Business*, March 4, 2019, https://www.chicagobusiness.com/health-care/new-walgreens-program-blurs-lines-between-pharmacy-retail.

6. A. Waytz and M. I. Norton, "Botsourcing and Outsourcing: Robot, British, Chinese, and German Workers Are for Thinking—Not Feeling—Jobs," *Emotion* 14, no. 2 (April 2014): 434–444.

7. R. Kottenstette, "Elon Musk Wasn't Wrong About Automating the Model 3 Assembly Line—He Was Just Ahead of His Time," *TechCrunch*, March 5, 2019, https://techcrunch.com/2019/03/05/elon-musk-wasnt-wrong-about-automating-the-model-3-assembly-line-he-was-just-ahead-of-his-time/.

8. J. R. Hackman and G. R. Oldham, "Development of the Job Diagnostic Survey," *Journal of Applied Psychology* 60, no. 2 (April 1975): 159–170.

9. For instance, a recent study of auditors showed that those who were randomly assigned to multitask were less able to identify existing errors in the auditing process. See C. E. Mullis and R. C. Hatfield, "The Effects of Multitasking on Auditors' Judgment Quality," *Contemporary Accounting Research* 35, no. 1 (spring 2018): 314–333.

10. C. Connley, "This Company Has an Ingenious Way to Free Employees from Email on Vacation," *CNBC*, updated August 17, 2017, https://www.cnbc.com/2017/08/17/one-companys-genius-way-to-free-employees-from-email-on-vacation.html.

11. H. A. White and P. Shah, "Creative Style and Achievement in Adults with Attention-Deficit/Hyperactivity Disorder," *Personality and Individual Differences* 50, no. 5 (April 2011): 673–677.

12. B. Baird, J. Smallwood, M. D. Mrazek, et al., "Inspired by Distraction: Mind Wandering Facilitates Creative Incubation," *Psychological Science* 23, no. 10 (August 2012): 1117–1122.

13. M. L. Meyer, H. E. Hershfield, A. Waytz, et al., "Creative Expertise Is Associated with Transcending the Here and Now," *Journal of Personality and Social Psychology* 116, no. 4 (April 2019): 483–494.

Chapter 3

1. W. Thomson, *Popular Lectures and Addresses*, vol. 1 (New York: Macmillan, 1889), 73.

2. A. L. Duckworth, C. Peterson, M. D. Matthews, and D. R. Kelly, "Grit: Perseverance and Passion for Long-Term Goals," *Journal of Personality and Social Psychology* 92, no. 6 (June 2007): 1087–1101.

3. A. L. Duckworth and P. D. Quinn, "Development and Validation of the Short Grit Scale (Grit-S)," *Journal of Personality Assessment* 91, no. 2 (February 2009): 166–174.

4. L. Eskreis-Winkler, J. J. Gross, and A. L. Duckworth, "Grit: Sustained Self-Regulation in the Service of Superordinate Goals," in *Handbook of Self-Regulation: Research, Theory, and Applications* (New York: Guilford, 2016).

5. Duckworth et al., "Grit: Perseverance and Passion"; A. L. Duckworth, T. A. Kirby, E. Tsukayama, et al., "Deliberate Practice Spells Success: Why Grittier Competitors Triumph at the National Spelling Bee," *Social Psychological and Personality Science* 2, no. 2 (March 2011): 174–181; and K. R. Von Culin, E. Tsukayama, and A. L. Duckworth, "Unpacking Grit: Motivational Correlates of Perseverance and Passion for Long-Term Goals," *Journal of Positive Psychology* 9, no. 4 (March 2014): 306–312.

6. R. Pausch, *The Last Lecture* (Hyperion, 2008).

7. A. Furnham, "The Great Divide: Academic Versus Practitioner Criteria for Psychometric Test Choice," *Journal of Personality Assessment* 100, no. 5 (September 2007): 498–506.

8. G. J. Fitzsimons, J. W. Hutchinson, P. Williams, et al., "Non-conscious Influences on Consumer Choice," *Marketing Letters* 13, no. 3 (August 2002): 269–279.

9. M. Snyder, "Self-Monitoring of Expressive Behavior," *Journal of Personality and Social Psychology* 30, no. 4 (October 1974): 526–537; L. E. Burke, J. Wang, and M. A. Sevick, "Self-Monitoring in Weight Loss: A Systematic Review of the Literature," *Journal of the American Dietetic Association* 111, no. 1 (January 2011): 92–102; R. K. Hester and H. D. Delaney, "Behavioral Self-Control Program for Windows: Results of a Controlled Clinical Trial," *Journal of Consulting and Clinical Psychology* 65, no. 4 (August 1997): 686–693; and B. J. Zimmerman and A. S. Paulsen, "Self-Monitoring During Collegiate Studying: An Invaluable Tool for Academic Self-Regulation," *New Directions for Teaching & Learning* 63 (fall 1995): 13–27.

10. D. Quinlan, N. Swain, and D. A. Vella-Brodrick, "Character Strength Interventions: Building on What We Know for Improved Outcomes," *Journal of Happiness Studies* 13, no. 6 (December 2012): 1145.

Chapter 4

1. See M. Bidwell, "Paying More to Get Less: The Effects of External Hiring Versus Internal Mobility," *Administrative Science Quarterly* 56, no. 3 (2011): 369–407; and P. S. DeOrtentiis, C. H. Van Iddekinge, R. E. Ployhart, et al., "Build or Buy? The Individual and Unit-Level Performance of Internally Versus Externally Selected Managers over Time," *Journal of Applied Psychology* 103, no. 8 (August 2018): 916–928.

2. For more details, see N. Guenole and S. Feinzig, "The Business Case for AI in HR," white paper, IBM Smarter Workforce Institute, Armonk, New York, November 2018, https://www.ibm.com/talent-management/ai-in-hr-business-case/.

3. Research by Shinjae Won at the University of Illinois at Urbana–Champaign reached a similar conclusion, showing that finalists for executive roles at nonprofits were more likely to get the job if they had broader functional experience. See S. Won, "Essays on Executive Search" (PhD diss., University of Pennsylvania, 2016).

Chapter 5

1. F. Schmidt, "The Validity and Utility of Selection Methods in Personnel Psychology: Practical and Theoretical Implications of 100 Years of Research Findings," working paper, University of Iowa, October 2016.

2. T. F. Bainbridge, J. A. Quinlan, R. A. Mar, et al., "Openness/Intellect and Susceptibility to Pseudo-Profound Bullshit: A Replication and Extension," *European Journal of Personality*, October 9, 2018.

3. W. Fleeson and E. Jayawickreme, "Whole Trait Theory," *Journal of Research in Personality* 56 (June 2015): 82–92.

4. W. Fleeson, "Toward a Structure- and Process-Integrated View of Personality: Traits as Density Distributions of States," *Journal of Personality and Social Psychology* 80, no. 6 (June 2011): 1011–1027.

5. J. D. Karpicke and J. R. Blunt, "Retrieval Practice Produces More Learning Than Elaborative Studying With Concept Mapping," *Science* 331, no. 6018 (February 11, 2011): 772–775.

6. J. J. A. Denissen, M. Luhmann, J. M. Chung, et al., "Transactions between Life Events and Personality Traits across the Adult Lifespan," *Journal of Personality and Social Psychology*, July 2018.

7. A. A. Minbashian, R. E. Wood, and N. Beckmann, "Task-Contingent Conscientiousness as a Unit of Personality at Work," *Journal of Applied Psychology* 95, no. 5 (September 2010): 793–806.

8. B. Little, "Who Are You, Really? The Puzzle of Personality," TED Talk, February 2016, https://www.ted.com/talks/brian_little_who_are_you_really_the_puzzle_of_personality.

9. L. K. Kammrath, R. Mendoza-Denton, and W. Mischel, "Incorporating If . . . Then . . . Personality Signatures in Person Perception: Beyond the Person-Situation Dichotomy," *Journal of Personality and Social Psychology* 88, no. 4 (April 2005): 605–618.

10. J. P. Green, R. S. Dalal, K. L. Swigart, et al., "Personality Consistency and Situational Influences on Behavior," *Journal of Management*, June 21, 2018.

Chapter 6

1. D. Gherson, B. Hancock, and A. Tavis, "Make It Personal: Lessons from IBM on Reinventing Performance Management," *MIT Sloan Management Review* webinar, April 17, 2019, https://sloanreview.mit.edu/video/webinar-lessons-from-ibm-on-reinventing-performance-management/.

Chapter 7

1. J. Chen, "Blind Loyalty: How a Social Network Is Redefining the Future of Corporate Culture," *TechCrunch*, August 11, 2018, https://techcrunch.com/2018/08/11/blind-loyalty/.

2. S. Snow, "My Company Is Killing Anonymous Employee Feedback: Here's Why," *Fast Company*, January 27, 2018, https://www.fastcompany.com/40518499/my-company-is-killing-anonymous-employee-feedback-heres-why.

3. G. C. Kane, D. Palmer, A. N. Philips, et al., "Aligning the Organization for Its Digital Future," *MIT Sloan Management Review*, July 26, 2016, https://sloanreview.mit.edu/projects/aligning-for-digital-future/.

4. V. Kumar and A. Pansari, "Measuring the Benefits of Employee Engagement," *MIT Sloan Management Review* 56, no. 4 (summer 2016): 67–72.

Chapter 8

1. "Udemy In Depth: 2018 Workplace Distraction Report," Udemy for Business, February 2018, https://research.udemy.com/research_report/udemy-depth-2018-workplace-distraction-report/.

Chapter 10

1. L. L. Greer, B. A. de Jong, M. E. Schouten, et al., "Why and When Hierarchy Impacts Team Effectiveness: A Meta-Analytic Integration," *Journal of Applied Psychology* 103, no. 6 (June 2018): 591–613.

2. F. R. C. de Wit, L. L. Greer, and K. A. Jehn, "The Paradox of Intra-group Conflict: A Meta-Analysis," *Journal of Applied Psychology* 97, no. 2 (March 2012): 360–390.

3. A. Groth, "Is Holacracy the Future of Work or a Management Cult?" October 9, 2018, https://qz.com/work/1397516/is-holacracy-the-future-of-work-or-a-management-cult/.

Chapter 12

1. Order of authorship is alphabetical, as this was a fully collaborative effort (although without analytics).

2. R. Cross, S. Taylor, and D. Zehner, "Collaboration without Burnout," *Harvard Business Review* 96, no. 4 (July–August 2018): 134–137; and R. Cross, R. Rebele, and A. Grant, "Collaborative Overload," *Harvard Business Review* 94, no. 1 (January–February 2016): 74–79.

3. R. Friedman, "The Cost of Continuously Checking Email," July 4, 2014, https://hbr.org/2014/07/the-cost-of-continuously-checking-email.

4. M. Lewis, "The No-Stats All-Star," *New York Times*, February 13, 2009, https://nyti.ms/2k5hskW.

5. B. Schoenfeld, "How Data (and Some Breathtaking Soccer) Brought Liverpool to the Cusp of Glory," *New York Times*, May 22, 2019, https://www.nytimes.com/2019/05/22/magazine/soccer-data-liverpool.html.

6. Others have approached this field more technically, by focusing on the metrics themselves. For instance, see P. Leonardi and N. Contractor, "Better People Analytics," *Harvard Business Review* 96, no. 6 (November–December 2018): 70–81. Our focus is on the problems that collaboration analytics can solve, in hopes of inspiring action among leaders who

need to understand more viscerally what impacts are possible before diving into the methods and metrics.

7. J. W. Boudreau and P. M. Ramstad, "Where's Your Pivotal Talent?" *Harvard Business Review* 83, no. 4 (April 2005): 23–24.

8. M. Mortensen and H. K. Gardner, "The Overcommitted Organization," *Harvard Business Review* 95, no. 5 (September–October 2017): 58–65.

9. M. J. Arena, *Adaptive Space: How GM and Other Companies Are Positively Disrupting Themselves and Transforming Into Agile Organizations* (New York: McGraw-Hill, 2018).

10. R. Cross and P. Gray, "Where Has the Time Gone? Addressing Collaboration Overload in a Networked Economy," *California Management Review* 56, no. 1 (fall 2013): 50–66.

11. G. Ballinger, E. Craig, R. Cross, et al., "A Stitch in Time Saves Nine: Leveraging Networks to Reduce the Costs of Turnover," *California Management Review* 53, no. 4 (summer 2011): 111–133.

12. R. Cross and R. J. Thomas, "Managing Yourself: A Smarter Way to Network," *Harvard Business Review* 89, no. 7–8 (July–August 2011): 149–155.

13. J. L. Whittington, S. Meskelis, E. K. Asare, et al., *Enhancing Employee Engagement: An Evidence-Based Approach* (New York: Palgrave Macmillan, 2017).

Chapter 13

1. Grand View Research, Team Collaboration Software Market Analysis Report, 2018, https://www.grandviewresearch.com/industry-analysis/team-collaboration-software-market.

2. L. A. Perlow, C. N. Hadley, and E. Eun, "Stop the Meeting Madness," *Harvard Business Review* 95, no. 4 (July–August 2017): 62–69.

3. M. Chui, J. Manyika, J. Bughin, et al., *The Social Economy: Unlocking Value and Productivity Through Social Technologies* (New York: McKinsey Global Institute, 2012): 46.

4. K. Sutcliffe and M. Barton, "Contextualized Engagement as Resilience-in-Action: A Study in Adventure Racing" (paper presented at the Academy of Management Annual Meeting, Chicago, Illinois, July 2018). Also see P. Ercolano, "'Resilience-in-Action' Is Key to Team Suc-

cess, Whether in Backwoods or Business," Johns Hopkins University, August 8, 2017, https://hub.jhu.edu/2017/08/08/backwoods-resilience -business-organizational-theory/.

5. F. Englmaier, S. Grimm, D. Schindler, et al., "The Effect of Incentives in Non-Routine Analytical Team Tasks—Evidence from a Field Experiment," working paper no. 6903, CESifo, Munich, Germany, February 21, 2018, https://papers.ssrn.com/sol3/papers.cfm?abstract_id=3164800.

6. It's somewhat surprising that more research hasn't been done on the social element of problem solving, given that scholars are increasingly discrediting the notion of the solo genius. See, for instance, K. Clark, "Myth of the Genius Solitary Scientist Is Dangerous," November 20, 2017, https://theconversation.com/myth-of-the-genius-solitary-scientist -is-dangerous-87835.

7. B. Uzzi, "Social Structure and Competition in Interfirm Networks: The Paradox of Embeddedness," *Administrative Science Quarterly* 42, no. 1 (1997): 35–67; R. S. Burt, "Structural Holes and Good Ideas," *American Journal of Sociology* 110, no. 2 (2004): 349–399; R. Cross and J. N. Cummings, "Tie and Network Correlates of Individual Performance in Knowledge-Intensive Work," *Academy of Management Journal* 47, no. 6 (2004): 928–937; and D. Lazer and A. Friedman, "The Network Structure of Exploration and Exploitation," *Administrative Science Quarterly* 52, no. 4 (2007): 667–694.

8. J. Shore, E. Bernstein, and D. Lazer, "Facts and Figuring: An Experimental Investigation of Network Structure and Performance in Information and Solution Spaces," *Organization Science* 26, no. 5 (2015): 1432–1446.

9. E. Bernstein, J. Shore, and D. Lazer, "How Intermittent Breaks in Interaction Improve Collective Intelligence," *Proceedings of the National Academy of Sciences* 115, no. 35 (2018): 8734–8739.

10. W. Mason and D. J. Watts, "Collaborative Learning in Networks," *Proceedings of the National Academy of Sciences* 109, no. 3 (2012): 764– 769; J. Lorenz, H. Rauhut, F. Schweitzer, et al., "How Social Influence Can Undermine the Wisdom of Crowd Effect," *Proceedings of the National Academy of Sciences* 108, no. 22 (2011): 9020–9025; and P. B. Paulus, V. L. Putman, K. L. Dugosh, et al., "Social and Cognitive Influences in

Group Brainstorming: Predicting Production Gains and Losses," *European Review of Social Psychology* 12, no. 1 (2002): 299–325.

11. K. J. Boudreau, N. Lacetera, and K. R. Lakhani, "Incentives and Problem Uncertainty in Innovation Contests: An Empirical Analysis," *Management Science* 57, no. 5 (2011): 843–863; and L. Hong and S. E. Page, "Groups of Diverse Problem Solvers Can Outperform Groups of High-Ability Problem Solvers," *Proceedings of the National Academy of Sciences* 101, no. 46 (2004): 16385–16389.

12. For instance, R. Cross and P. Gray, "Where Has the Time Gone? Addressing Collaboration Overload in a Networked Economy," *California Management Review* 56, no. 1 (2013): 50–66; R. Cross, R. Rebele, and A. Grant, "Collaborative Overload," *Harvard Business Review* 94, no. 1 (January–February 2016): 74–79; and R. Cross, S. Taylor, and D. Zehner, "Collaboration without Burnout," *Harvard Business Review* 96, no. 4 (July–August 2018): 134–137. For a different manifestation of the same issue, see T. L. Stanko and C. M. Beckman, "Watching You Watching Me: Boundary Control and Capturing Attention in the Context of Ubiquitous Technology Use," *Academy of Management Journal* 58, no. 3 (2014): 712–738.

13. At BCG, each consultant was required to have one scheduled night off per week, and productivity improved. See L. A. Perlow and J. L. Porter, "Making Time Off Predictable—and Required," *Harvard Business Review* 87, no. 10 (October 2009): 102–109.

14. L. A. Perlow, "The Time Famine: Toward a Sociology of Work Time," *Administrative Science Quarterly* 44, no. 1 (1999): 57–81.

15. S. Ghosh and A. Wu, "Iterative Coordination in Organizational Search," working paper, Harvard Business School, Cambridge, Massachusetts, January 2019.

16. H. Ibarra and M. Hansen, "Are You a Collaborative Leader?" *Harvard Business Review* 89, no. 7–8 (July–August 2011): 68–74.

17. R. Singer, "Hand Over Responsibility," chap. 9 in *Shape Up: Stop Running in Circles and Ship Work That Matters*, accessed July 15, 2019, https://basecamp.com/shapeup/3.1-chapter-09.

18. P. Leonardi and N. Contractor, "Better People Analytics," *Harvard Business Review* 96, no. 6 (November–December 2018): 70–81.

19. L. A. Perlow, *Sleeping With Your Smartphone: How to Break the 24/7 Habit and Change the Way You Work* (Boston: Harvard Business Review Press, 2012).

20. See, for instance, C. Newport, *Deep Work: Rules for Focused Success in a Distracted World* (London: Hachette, 2016); and N. Carr, *The Shallows: What the Internet Is Doing to Our Brains* (New York: Norton, 2010).

Chapter 16

1. R. Hogan, T. Chamorro-Premuzic, and R. B. Kaiser, "Employability and Career Success: Bridging the Gap between Theory and Reality," *Industrial and Organizational Psychology* 6, no. 1 (March 2013): 3–16.

2. T. Chamorro-Premuzic, D. Winsborough, R. A. Sherman, et al., "New Talent Signals: Shiny New Objects or a Brave New World?" *Industrial and Organizational Psychology* 9, no. 3 (September 2016): 621–640.

3. J. Bersin, "HR Technology Disruptions for 2018: Productivity, Design, and Intelligence Reign," Bersin by Deloitte, 2017.

4. N. Perveen, N. Ahmad, M. Abdul Qadoos Bilal Khan, et al., "Facial Expression Recognition through Machine Learning," *International Journal of Scientific and Technology Research* 5, no. 4 (March 2016): 91–97.

5. C. P. Latha and M. M. Priya, "A Review on Deep Learning Algorithms for Speech and Facial Emotion Recognition," *International Journal of Control Theory and Applications* 9, no. 24 (January 2016): 183–204.

6. G. Park, H. A. Schwartz, J. C. Eichstaedt, et al., "Automatic Personality Assessment through Social Media Language," *Journal of Personality and Social Psychology* 108, no. 6 (June 2015): 934–952.

7. G. Farnadi, G. Sitaraman, S. Sushmita, et al., "Computational Personality Recognition in Social Media," *User Modeling and User-Adapted Interaction* 26, no. 2–3 (June 2016).

8. L. M. Hough, F. L. Oswald, and R. E. Ployhart, "Determinants, Detection, and Amelioration of Adverse Impact in Personnel Selection Procedures: Issues, Evidence, and Lessons Learned," *International Journal of Selection and Assessment* 9, no. 1–2 (March 2001): 152–194.

Chapter 18

1. "Warner Re-Introduces Bills to Prepare Americans for the Future of Work," press release, February 25, 2019, https://www.warner.senate .gov/public/index.cfm/2019/2/warner-re-introduces-bills-to-prepare -americans-for-the-future-of-work.

2. R. Miller and M. A. McCarthy, "The Future of Workplace Learning, Skills, and Economic Mobility," New America blog post, December 2, 2018, https://www.newamerica.org/education-policy/edcentral/future -workplace-learning-skills-and-economic-mobility/.

Index